# A Little Piece of Heaven

Alison Hill

The author has represented and warranted full ownership and/or legal right to publish all the materials in this book.

A Little Piece of Heaven
All Rights Reserved.
Copyright © 2012 Alison Hill
ISBN:978-0-9574999-0-4
www.alisonhill-author.co.uk/
In His Glory Publishing
All scripture quotations are taken from the Holy Bible, New International Version, unless otherwise indicated.

Cover Photo © 2012 JupiterImages Corporation. All rights reserved

- used with permission.

This book may not be reproduced, transmitted, or stored in whole or in part by any means, including graphic, electronic, or mechanical without the express written consent of the publisher/author except in the case of brief quotations embodied in critical articles and reviews.

# Contents

| | |
|---|---:|
| Introduction | 1 |
| Acknowledgement | 3 |
| It's a Question of Choice | 5 |
| Wisdom for the Journey | 9 |
| Encountering Wisdom | 19 |
| A Lake of Delights | 29 |
| Dreams, Faces and Forgiveness | 41 |
| The Cave | 47 |
| Dancing with the King | 57 |
| Mending the Nets | 63 |
| A Very Special Occasion | 73 |
| Higher Up the Mountain | 81 |
| A New Place | 89 |
| Rubies, Diamonds and Hidden Treasures | 99 |
| Things are not what they seem! | 107 |
| The Call and the Cost | 111 |
| A Canopy Under the Stars | 119 |
| God's Chosen Vessels | 123 |
| A Sea of Faces | 129 |
| The Throne Room | 135 |

| | |
|---|---:|
| Ministering Spirits, a Golden Door and a Chance Encounter with a Great Man of God | 143 |
| Angels on Assignment | 153 |
| The Garden of Remembrance | 163 |
| A Place of Regret and Triumph! | 171 |

# Introduction

Many of us at some time or another have wondered what heaven is like. Our thoughts can get lost in eternity and what it would be like to live forever. This book tries to capture a glimpse of this future. Some aspects will be familiar and can be found in Scripture, whilst others are part of my imagination. But either way this book will cause you to think some more about what your journey to heaven would be like; including how your life on earth will influence your future. I have brought some teaching points into the book which I hope you will benefit from (these are highlighted in italics). The journey begins with a choice and it is a choice which all of us have to make. Do we walk with our creator on the journey that He has set before us or do we go our own way? A Little Piece of Heaven shows you the results of some of the choices we have made on our journey through life. For me, this journey has resulted in a close walk with God; through this walk I have learnt to rely on Him; believing His voice in all circumstances. The essence of this book has come from all that I have learnt about God and His ways.

## A LITTLE PIECE OF HEAVEN

Let us submit our lives to the King of Heaven.

"For God so loved the world that he gave his one and only Son, that whoever believes in him shall not perish but have eternal life."

John 3:16

# Acknowledgement

I would like to express my gratitude to my mother, Glenys Mills and my mother-in-law, Louise Hill, for their love and support in the production of my books.

I thank God for prompting me to write a book that would have never been attempted, without His encouragement and gifting. I am amazed at how God has developed my faith over many years enabling me to write books with the inspiration of the Holy Spirit. I would like to acknowledge the blessing that my two children, Rebecca and Adrian, have been over the years.

# It's a Question of Choice

As I sat meekly at the foot of the mountain I looked up and saw God at the top in all of His glory and majesty.

"How am I *ever* going to get up there or anywhere near His presence? Should I begin this journey or turn back?"

These were the questions that raced through my mind. To turn back meant defeat and I was not one to give in that easily. To stay where I was seemed futile and a waste; there was only one answer which was to move forward. What would I find on my journey? I could ask God what the journey would entail, but what would I do with this knowledge? Would it create even more choices and complicate my responses?

A mist began to descend at the top of the mountain and God faded into the distance. Did this mean that my time for choice was limited or was I simply being ushered into making a decision? *Moving forward meant change and suffering for the sake of the Gospel; it was the choice all believers must make, unless we turn back when the journey becomes tough.*

Slowly the mist lifted and I saw a smile on the face of God, as if I had already made my choice. In fact — I had. As I searched my heart, I realised that God had heard my heart rather than my words. A peace descended as I rose to my feet and walked up the mountain. I was so excited at the prospect of getting closer to God that I quickly forgot where I was and felt the strain of going up rather than the ease of where I had been. I felt a sense of trepidation as I left the past behind and stepped into my future.

I started to look back and then stopped as I remembered the story of Lot's wife, who looked back longingly at the city she had once lived in and subsequently turned to stone. I recognised that my heart was compelling me to do the same. *The known is sometimes safer than the unknown; less exciting but safe. A battle will always rage in our hearts when our flesh cries out for the security we once had.* A change began to take place within; feelings of insecurity echoed around my mind. It felt as if the Tectonic plates of my being were beginning to shift, causing an internal earthquake. I didn't like this feeling and in the same way volcanoes and mountains are forged naturally, something was beginning to change within me, causing me to fear. My values were being challenged and I found myself looking at God in a different way. I wanted God to take away this awful feeling and replace it with peace. But the more I stared at God the more desperate I felt.

I cried out, "Do something God, do something, take away this feeling of being lost."

God gazed in my direction with a reassuring smile as if He was saying that everything was alright. But it wasn't; I felt lost and frightened. As I fell to my feet with a sense of failure so early into the journey, a voice inside of me said,

"Where does your trust lie? Is it in Me and My promises, or is it in what you have known? If it is in Me, then you must confess with your mouth and believe in your heart."

> "For it is with your heart that you believe and are justified, and it is with your mouth that you confess and are saved."

> Romans 10:10

As the tears that had streamed down my face dried up, I spoke out words of faith. The voice of the enemy within raged like a roaring lion.

"Give in, this won't work." The lion roared. "You are as you feel. Nothing can change the way you feel. This is not where you belong."

But the voice of faith grew louder and said,

"Speak it out, now, if you believe!"

As words of faith poured out of my mouth, nothing changed within. I thought about all the times people had told me of God being true to His word. Faith began to take hold of me and I repeated words of trust in God many times before a glimmer of hope broke through. Even though I felt weak, I rose to my feet and walked forward *because faith without action is dead*. My steps grew stronger with every move. Nothing had changed within me, but my heart was resolute. I was determined to trust in God regardless of the way my flesh was trying to drag me back into a place of defeat.

As I walked forward, the atmosphere around me changed and the presence of God surrounded me. The hours passed and as the night descended the guiding light of God increased. My heart grew strong: *I could see that faith requires a lot of effort at times, even when our circumstances have not changed.* I decided to lie down for the night and ponder what I had learnt that day as I was determined not to forget. There would be many more occasions during which this lesson of faith would prove to be invaluable, not only for me, but for those I would meet on my journey through life. I was passionate about sharing the treasures of the Kingdom of God. A deep sleep came upon me and the mist I had seen on the mountain at the beginning of my journey had now descended and swamped me with the peace of God. I slept soundly that night and I realised that the steps of obedience that I had started to take had many rewards.

# Wisdom for the Journey

I awoke the next morning with a sense of anticipation which was quickly shattered by the noise of many voices around me. As I looked around, I saw that I was not alone on this journey. I was surrounded by many that were also facing the mountain and had agreed to move forward into the purposes of God. I suddenly paled into what I thought was insignificance as the day before had been about my unique relationship with God. I selfishly thought that I was the only one on this wonderful journey. I humbled myself to acknowledge that the heart of God was for all of mankind to each have a unique journey through life; not just me. I wondered where the people had all come from and why I hadn't seen them yesterday. This sea of faces had only become visible as God had opened my eyes to unseen realities. I was yet to discover many more of these unseen realities, but first of all I needed to know how to relate to others who were on the same journey as me. As I looked, smiles began to break out on their faces and a realisation came over us all that we needed each other for this long and difficult journey. *God has designed us so that we need each other and our unique gifts become a necessity to help one another in our journey through life.* This reminded me of many times at church when the

Body of Christ was preached in a way that proved we all needed each other.

I stared at the masses and I wondered how I would make my way to the people whom God had destined me to be with at this particular stage of my journey. How would I know who they were and what certainty did I have that we would relate to one another? After all, I have not got anything in common with these people, other than our faith in Jesus Christ.

As I walked into the crowd the people began to separate and a small group walked closer to me. A clear distinction emerged between those closest to me and those far off. It was as though their faces were shining on me. Warmth entered my heart as one by one, they spoke to me. I then realised that it is God who chooses those that will help us on our journey; only He can connect us. As I talked with them, I realised that these people were going to be on the same journey as me and I wanted to learn as much as I could from them before I climbed any higher.

A cold wind swirled around me and the warmth of the people closest to me began to fade and there didn't seem to be time to enjoy their company. I turned around as their faces faded and the blizzard that ensued caused me to only see what was immediately in front of me. I didn't like to have such limited vision but regardless, I moved forward. My footsteps were unsure and fearful; the ground beneath became rough and the terrain difficult to tackle.

"How could I go from a moment of peace and security into a place of such difficulty, when I have done nothing wrong?" I thought. It was then a voice came out of the blizzard,

"What was in your heart before the blizzard began?"

As I searched my heart and retraced my feelings, I could see that the moment God had placed these people around me; my heart had taken a change of direction. I had thought that these people were going to be more important than God on my journey and a sense of dependency had entered my heart.

I couldn't understand how this had happened as I didn't consciously make that decision. I recalled this piece of Scripture.

"The heart is deceitful above all things and beyond cure. Who can understand it?"

Jeremiah 17:9

I sank to my knees. How was I ever going to survive a journey in which I could so easily fall from the path of righteousness? It felt impossible; I had only just started and felt I had failed again. Before I had spoken words of repentance, these Scriptures came to mind.

"Love the LORD your God with all your heart and with all your soul and with all your strength."

Deuteronomy 6:5

"You shall have no other gods before me."

Exodus 20:3

The feelings of failure quickly washed away as the grace of God poured over me. My pride was replaced by humility, as well as an awareness of how easy it is to fall. As I rose to my feet, I felt I could raise my eyes again and look at the One who was the lover of my soul. The blizzard had completely gone and was replaced with sunshine, birdsong and a decision on my behalf to put God first in my heart. Making sure that to spend time with Him; seeking His face was the most important part of my life.

As I walked with Him in this wonderful garden that had begun to appear, I realised that nature itself had suddenly become alive in His presence. Not only did God bring life to human beings, but even nature was transformed into all of its glory. The plants swayed in the cool night air and the colours of the leaves were transformed by the evening light that rested on their waxy surface. I had never looked at plants so closely, noticing the array of shades that came with each one and how each plant could contain such unique designs.

As I walked in the garden, I realised that there were no dying plants and the radiance of the colours far outshone anything I had seen in my world. Even though I felt completely at home in this place with feelings of peace that were beyond my expectations; I was aware that this was not my home, I was a visitor. I looked up and saw a serene smile on the face of my Creator. I knew that He had brought me to this place for reasons which were beyond my present ability to comprehend. I was so excited by the prospect of this unique calling that I quickly forgot the faces of the friends that God had shown me; it made me realise how fickle humans can be. *One minute we feel overwhelmed with a particular desire but when the presence of God truly takes His place in our lives, we don't want anything else.* I was incredibly content in this place and I didn't care about anything or anybody; this was where I wanted to stay - forever. What joy entered my heart! I could spend eternity simply getting to know my Creator with no distractions and no heartache. There were no words exchanged and I had no desire to speak as I walked through this exquisite garden. I simply knew what God was saying and His presence was all I needed. What bliss, there was no effort; no questions asked about the world and all of its pain. All that I thought I would ask simply faded away; those questions were of no significance now.

As dusk became night a voice broke the silence;

"Don't settle here My child; you will have to go back to earth soon. You can't remain in this place. What I have shown you is for you to share with those you will meet on earth."

Tears rolled down my cheeks; hardness entered my heart. This hardness was a self-centeredness that meant I was beginning to think only of myself. Thoughts began to race through my mind.

"Why should I return? I really don't want to; there is nothing the world can give me that can compare with what I have found here."

God's reply caused me to shudder with embarrassment.

"Is your life all about you; is your motive for living about what the world can give you or for that matter what I can give you? Your answer proves that you need to go back to become a giver and to think of others more than yourself."

I again found myself on my knees with a realisation that my heart was deceitful. The journey of change that was ahead of me seemed more than I could bear. I had such a lack of wisdom and understanding of the ways and purposes of God, that I felt it would take me a lifetime to change my thinking.

As God heard my thoughts He replied,

"You know it doesn't take a lifetime for you to change your thinking. It simply takes humility to know that your life requires you to ask for wisdom at every stage of your journey. To be aware of your inclination to move into your own fleshly thoughts and ideas at any time of every day should cause you to submit your thoughts to Me and to allow My wisdom to become yours. To train your mind to think in this way takes time, so do not be too hard on yourself. You need to be transformed by the renewing of your mind, but to do it is a process which will take all of your life. All you have to do is to decide to submit *your* ways and humbly accept that Mine are perfect."

"Do not conform any longer to the pattern of this world, but be transformed by the renewing of your mind. Then you will be able to test and approve what God's will is — his good, pleasing and perfect will."

Romans 12:2

I was about to give Jesus lordship over my own thoughts and my own ideas. Did this mean I would lose my own identity in the process and never have a unique idea that was mine alone? Did this mean that once I took the step of allowing all of God's wisdom to replace my own, I would no longer be allowed to take any of the credit for the things I did? I would have to admit to friends, family and church members that all my plans were God's idea. I have to admit that I liked the thought of getting a pat on the back or a round of applause now and again. Surely to give it all up for God to get all the glory would be too much. I then thought of Solomon and the book of Ecclesiastes. Solomon appeared to be the most successful of all of the kings. He achieved all that he wanted to achieve and owned everything any person could ever want. He received praise from the leaders of nations, such as the Queen of Sheba and so his fame spread. All that God required of him was to be obedient to the ways of God and to trust that His ways were perfect. Unfortunately, Solomon decided to have many wives from nations in which God had told him not to intermarry because they would turn his heart to other gods. The book of Ecclesiastes was written after Solomon realised that God's ways were the only way to live; he had learnt the consequences of straying from these truths. Using God's wisdom would have protected him in his kingship and his life. After reading these somewhat depressing chapters, I took with me a sense that *nothing will bring us joy and peace unless we are completely submitted to God and His ways.*

"Let it go..." a voice echoed. "Is it worth exchanging the lie of the world for the truth of God?"

"What is it that I am being asked to let go of?" I thought. "Pride," came the reply.

As I thought about this I realised that this did not require any consideration, I either trust in God or I don't. I remembered that while I was in the presence of God it didn't enter my head to achieve anything because I was completely satisfied with Him. I gave God my answer with a heart that had been transformed.

"With all of my heart I choose to follow you O Lord: I

submit to Your ways and Your wisdom."

A light poured over me. From that moment on I felt lightness in my spirit. I realised that this decision had caused a burden to lift off me; a burden that I had carried all of my life and one which seemed to be a normal part of our lives on earth. The burden was the responsibility to make right decisions: *a burden that has been carried by mankind since the beginning of the fall of man. God released Adam and Eve from His wisdom in the Garden of Eden and allowed them to be the rulers of their own destiny. With it came a great burden and great sin.*

"You see," said God, "Man was never meant to be alone in decision making. I gave him Godly wisdom to flow naturally from his mind, but when Adam and Eve made the decision to sin, they separated themselves from My order. Through their actions, they were letting Me know that they felt able to make their own decisions in life."

A shudder ran down my spine as I realised that *the very thing we think is independence, actually causes us to carry a great burden. Decision making should have been so simple and yet we have made it so hard.* I thought of the times that I have walked carefree along the beach whilst on holiday; I had felt the peace of God and the peace of life. Just for a short while I had no cares for the present or the future: in that moment I got a glimpse of how life should have been. *We think that we will be happier when we get all that we long for and yet the happiest moments of my life have been when I have had nothing. No possessions, no cares and no responsibilities, which is what God intended when He created us. As I realised that nothing would change until Christ returned, I resigned myself to accepting that mankind has to continually submit its ways and its thinking to God. The treasure map for our life is found in the hands of the Master; it is only He that can bless our days as we align our lives with His will.*

As the light dimmed, peace entered my heart and as each truth of life was brought to my attention, I could see that the journey I was on was going to last a life-time. My peace came from knowing that I was not alone, nor would I ever be. God would always be there with the answers to my life and the answers for those that followed Him.

"Jesus answered, 'I am the way and the truth and the life. No-one comes to the Father except through me.'"

John 14:6

# Encountering Wisdom

The day passed by quickly and as the evening came I sat in front of a warm, glowing fire. The night air began to feel damp and cold: I drew close as I looked up into the darkening sky, seeing a dim reflection of the last rays of sunshine hitting the shores of the lake in front of me and as the rays danced on the water, a mist began to rise. I was glad that I had been given a deeper sense of security in God, which would bring me the peace that I needed in my life. I lay on the bed that had been prepared especially for me and I breathed a deep sigh of contentment as I watched the reflections on the lake for a little while longer; until the peace that consumed me caused me to sleep.

The next morning, I heard the shrill sound of birdsong enter my ears as if it was purposefully waking me up. Having no idea what time of day it was, I jumped to my feet to find the sun was shining and the dampness of the night air had been dried up by the sun's rays. I wondered what was in store for me today and what treasures would I find that would take me that much closer to the God of the universe.

I turned around to see a figure looming over me. With a startled look, I asked him his name and who he was. The man replied,

## A LITTLE PIECE OF HEAVEN

"I am your guide for today and I do not have a title. I find that names and titles complicate things; they cause humans to limit ability. In this place they are unnecessary because we all play the role to which we have been assigned for that day."

I looked at his face and a smile broke out on what had otherwise been an expressionless countenance.

"Don't worry." the man said, "I often cause confusion to those that I meet, but I can assure you that as today passes you will come to understand me better."

I turned and looked around, wondering where he had come from and if there were any more people to meet. The man beckoned me to walk with him; he walked quickly and every second step he gave a skip. He was peculiar but also very likeable and I felt that I was going to enjoy his company. As I caught him up, he realised that it would be better for both of us if he slowed down to my pace.

"Are you hungry?" I was asked. "Very." I replied.

I looked around and saw nothing that looked remotely edible. I had hoped for a three course meal that would exceed my expectations! The man heard my heart and told me that he was hoping that I would have been more excited to learn about God. I remembered the story of Jesus in the desert when He was tempted by Satan offering Him food.

> "Jesus answered, 'It is written: 'Man does not live on bread alone, but on every word that comes from the mouth of God.'"
>
> Matthew 4:4

## ENCOUNTERING WISDOM

The man asked me if I understood this Scripture and I admitted that my knowledge of its meaning was limited. The man explained how important it was to feed your soul with the Word of God and how it was more necessary than earthly food.

"The soul is *always* hungry; it's just a question of what you feed it with. If you feed it well, you will never be in want, but feeding your soul with the wrong food can lead to destruction."

Suddenly my natural hunger pains left me and I wanted to know more.

"How can I automatically know what to feed my soul?"

"Whatever is good, pure and lovely." He replied.

I found this difficult, living in a world where sin was at every door and wherever you turned, you were tainted with a worldly view on life and living. It didn't seem possible, unless I shut myself away on a desert island somewhere. Hearing my thoughts the man showed me that to try to live a life of purity required much discipline and trust. I wondered why trust would have to play such a big role and I was surprised at the answer coming from within. I could see that I was beginning to allow wisdom to play its part within my soul, rather than asking my guide. I realised that in order to give up what everyone else seemed to be enjoying, I needed to trust that God would fill the void with something much better. I was thrilled at these profound truths being so accessible, by simply waiting for the Holy Spirit to show me the answer through the wisdom of God. Most of my life had been filled with a lack of confidence; I avoided making decisions that might have had a bad effect on my life.

## A LITTLE PIECE OF HEAVEN

Staleness had overtaken; I had become stationary; unable to move forward for fear of making a wrong move. With this new found wisdom of God, anything became possible and I realised I could do anything!

The man I was walking with suddenly went out of sight and my footsteps ground to a halt with this new revelation.

"Wait for me!" I shouted.

As the man turned and looked in my direction, I saw that his face had become serious and concerned.

"What's wrong?" I asked.

"Do you think that wisdom is to be used for your own purposes and achievements, or for the purposes of God?" He replied.

Instead of the self pity that I had previously felt when being disciplined by God, I acknowledged my error and understood that *the wisdom of God was not for our benefit alone. His wisdom is not a tool to gain approval from others or to promote our life.* As I admitted my error a peace came to my soul as I realised that when our attitude is not right, we forfeit a level of peace. The peace that is forfeited goes unnoticed amid the excitement of selfish ambition and thoughts of self-promotion. How easily we forfeit the peace that could be ours for the cheap exchange of a lie.

> "What good will it be for a man if he gains
> the whole world, yet forfeits his soul? Or what
> can a man give in exchange for his soul?
>
> Matthew 16:26

## ENCOUNTERING WISDOM

*Prior to becoming a Christian our thought processes are governed by self.* I had to let go of this way of thinking, to truly know what it is to be a child of God. An understanding started to enter my mind of what promotion in the Kingdom was all about and with it came a greater ability to serve the needs of others. This understanding came with great responsibility. *Many of man's promotions have self at the forefront. The ultimate accolade is a title which means recognition and prestige for many. Even the most humble title brings recognition.* I remembered the Scripture,

"God said to Moses, 'I AM WHO I AM. This is what you are to say to the Israelites: 'I AM has sent me to you.'"

Exodus 3:14

I remembered what my guide had said when I first met him. I realised that the ultimate title we could have was none at all; *instead we should admit that with God in our lives, all titles are possible. This is the only true acknowledgment that we should be aiming for; that in and through Him we can do and be all things in any given situation. To strive for a particular title in life for security and recognition is the very thing that limits God's people from becoming all that they can be.*

The wisdom of God was beginning to take root in the very core of my being. As I looked ahead, the guide that had been with me for a relatively short time was now in the distance. As I shouted for him to wait, he turned and waved goodbye. I became sad as he faded into the distance, I wondered why he couldn't have stayed with me a while longer.

A voice within said,

"Here I am! I have been at your side, walking with you,

showing you the way; until you recognised that I am also within you and you can now hear the voice of wisdom wherever you are."

I was overwhelmed at the clarity with which I could now hear his voice, I realised the extent that God would speak into my life and just how close He was. I felt such a tremendous love for God; the tears began to flow as I sat down to enjoy this feeling of being loved. But at the same time I realised that I had gone throughout most of my life without this knowledge. My tears increased; the crying turned to weeping as I felt regret at the wasted years. How could I have gone through so many years without knowing this love, how foolish are so many that are blind to what I was blind to for so long? My weeping was coming from deep down inside; God was doing a cleansing work within, washing away the sadness in my soul and at the same time awakening me to the realities of my new life.

I suddenly felt strange as I was lifted up out of my body. Up, up, up I went and I soared higher as lightness in my spirit took over; joy filled my body as I was taken before God.

A voice echoed out of the light;

"What you consider loss is turned into gain in My Kingdom. For all the years you have not had the privilege of knowing Me and My inheritance, I transform into gain. As the deep regret takes hold of you, it produces fruit beyond what you could ever know. To make up for the years of loss, you develop a greater passion for the things of God and the call on your life. When you have lived a life without Me, your life with Me will have more meaning. You have experienced the world and you have tasted what it has to offer. You have tasted it and have found it wanting. It has left bitterness in the pit of your soul. Your hunger for Me has meant that you have been able to yield more fully. You have seen the shallowness of the world and you know that what I bring through My presence is by far the better choice. So you see My child that none of those years were wasted. You have eternity to enjoy the blessings of My Kingdom."

The regret I had felt melted away and the joy of knowing the Lord took its place. It was wonderful to think that I had eternity to enjoy my inheritance. I felt a deep gratitude for the sacrifice made and the suffering Jesus went through, which took on an even deeper meaning as I pondered the cross and its power to free mankind.

I would love to be able to show mankind what wonders they have in store for them, if they would only accept Jesus. *How can mankind ignore God and believe that we have been formed through evolution? Surely the complexity of our brains alone is enough to show even the greatest scientist that there must be a God. The greatest minds on earth have spent years developing cures for illness and developing technology to the place it is today. So how do intellectuals think that humans could have simply developed through a process of nature? If that is the case, mankind can sit back and wait for the great developments of science to simply happen without any effort. We cannot scientifically explain faith and yet we all recognise that it is a powerful tool in the life of a believer. In much the same way, the power of hope takes a person from a place of inactivity into a place of action. There are so many unexplainable things in the world; to accept God requires humility and an acceptance of the human limitation to understand and fathom the secrets of the Kingdom of God.*

## A LITTLE PIECE OF HEAVEN

I looked at my future without feelings of regret and with a sense of excitement about how God would use me in the lives of others. I became aware of my body again and as I looked down, I saw a reflection of myself in a pool of clear water. My countenance was beginning to change. The years that had taken their toll on my features were suddenly disappearing and a more youthful look was beginning to appear. I didn't realise how quickly life's difficulties could have an effect on my physical appearance. The pool of water looked inviting; I was beginning to get rather thirsty after all of the tears I had shed. I cupped my hands into the water and poured it down my throat. The water was refreshing and as I became satisfied and had my fill, I was aware of the icy water running through every part of my being. Freshness entered my soul as I experienced the crisp feeling of new emotions that I had never felt before; satisfying the deep recesses of my soul. I remembered this Scripture.

> "The LORD is my shepherd, I shall not be in want.
> He makes me lie down in green pastures,
> he leads me beside quiet waters,
> he restores my soul."

Psalm 23:1-2

"So this is what the restoring of a person's soul feels like." I thought.

God drew closer and said,

"My people see through a glass dimly. The truths of God, spoken of in My word are only experienced as a light breeze by many, instead of the full expression of the realities they hold. If My people knew how to tap into the deep truths of My word they would have more freedom. To ponder one truth alone and to understand its complete meaning could take a lifetime. Yet My children do not take the time to stay with one truth, before they move onto the next. They forfeit so much for the sake of being busy. My children think that to be busy in the church is the greatest sacrifice.

"But I tell you, that to spend time with Me, finding out the greatest truths of My word is by far the greater sacrifice. To truly know one truth in fullness, can mean the setting free of many tormented souls. My children are in such lack because of this; with so much running around with the appearance of being fruitful. They love to be in the presence of those who have yielded their lives to Me and display the glory of God. But instead of believing that they too can display the works of power, which are symbolic of a true son of God; they chase around from one meeting to the next: hungry for My Spirit, in the hope that they will have an amazing encounter with Me; propelling them forward in life and ministry. And yet they find few revelations that bring change."

I felt saddened, as I realised how much we miss out on because of the struggle to stay in His presence. And yet, I have done this very same thing again and again. *It is as if an alarm clock goes off inside and tells us to go and do something else, so we can feel that our day has been more fruitful. Most of what we do is fruitless, if we really look at it. Especially the time spent in front of the television or computer. If we really pondered the value of finding treasures of the Kingdom, we would not want to cut short our times with God. We would reap so much more from our day if we get our priorities right.*

## A LITTLE PIECE OF HEAVEN

*Distraction is all part of the devils plan to rob us of what is truly valuable: the greatest attacks come as subtle suggestions that lead to what we think is a good idea. Before we know it, we are distracted from God's best. To capture every thought is in Scripture for a reason, even though it seems such an extreme thing to do. The power of the mind is like a sail on a boat; it sets the course for our life.* This part of my life had to change, I did not want to let the enemy rob me of the best that God had for me. I suddenly felt a warmth wrap around me like a blanket; I could hear God saying,

"Be at peace, My child. You can only learn these truths one at a time and even though you see others who have already grasped what you are now learning, My grace is sufficient for you to learn it at a pace you can cope with."

# A Lake of Delights

I was drawn to the lake like a fish to water, so I decided to camp next to it for the night. The lake shimmered with many colours and as the light turned the colours into different shades, I was amazed at its beauty; I wondered if I would be allowed to swim in it. Wisdom was showing me that there was something contained within the lake that would amaze me and it was all I could do to contain my excitement. As I slept, I occasionally awoke like a child would do the night before their birthday, wondering what wonderful gifts were in store the next day. The lake glistened in the night air as the moon danced on the water. Even at night the colours were rich and mesmerizing.

I could not tell how deep these waters were, but it did not seem to matter. Throughout my life, I would only swim if I could see clearly to the bottom, but this time I knew that I would have no fear. I drifted off into a deep sleep with the most wonderful dreams of being overwhelmed by waves of the Holy Spirit depositing spiritual gifts from God. As I awoke and remembered the dreams, I was aware that God was preparing me to experience these gifts in the lake of delights. As the sun burst forth to introduce a new and exciting day, I welcomed it with open arms. I could not remember ever having a day

# A LITTLE PIECE OF HEAVEN

that I had embraced as much as this one.

As the warmth of the sun beckoned me to get ready for the day, I was not sure what I was going to do next.

The edge of the water rippled towards me, as if it was liquid gold lapping upon the shore. It rolled forward then back, forward then back and as I watched it, I felt it was enticing me to put my toes just on the edge. I wanted to be careful to be led by God in all that He had for me. I had been careless of this truth so many times. *When beckoned forward into the things of God, I had run ahead with the excitement of the moment and missed the fullness of what God had for me because the timing was wrong.* I was not prepared to miss out anymore and so I trod carefully at the water's edge waiting for the next move to be obvious. I remembered a piece of Scripture which confirmed my thoughts;

"Are you so foolish? After beginning with the Spirit, are you now trying to attain your goal by human effort?"

Galatians 3:3

*How can something so simple be so difficult for us to understand? Is it because of impatience? Do we become so excited by what is happening that we run ahead of God or is it that we don't really understand the concept of timing?* I was reminded of the Scripture;

"...because those who are led by the Spirit of God are sons of God."

Romans 8:14

The beauty of the day blessed my soul and as I looked into the water a reflection appeared. The reflection looked like Jesus and yet my face was blended into the image. I only wanted to see the face of Jesus and yet mine kept getting in the way. As I became frustrated, a voice spoke out of the reflection.

"Don't try to remove your face from Mine. Remember that you are made in My image and as time passes I shall become your most outstanding feature."

> "Now we see but a poor reflection as in a mirror; then we shall see face to face."
>
> 1 Corinthians 13:12

I was transfixed with this image and I found it hard to see my face contained in the face of Jesus, because deep down I didn't see myself reflecting His qualities.

Jesus spoke out of the reflection.

"Don't see yourself through your eyes; you must see yourself as I see you. Look how far you have come and know that for every challenge you face, I am with you. Do not look ahead because you will stumble. It is the journey that makes you who you will become. Value the journey and don't be frustrated by it. The journey is the process that equips you to become all that you can be, in Me.

"It is dangerous to think that you don't need the process. Those who think they can pass through, without examining their heart, are the ones in danger of falling quickly in their "success". What is their goal and why do they want to get to the end result so quickly? Is it because of success and ambition? I always look at the heart: to prepare a person properly I cause them to let go of their goal altogether. The purpose and direction of their life will fade into insignificance, as I work in their heart to purify their motives. The end result should only be to do what the Father wants them to do, at every stage of their life. That is their purpose. I call you to fix your eyes on the goal but until you realise that your goal is Me, your foundations will not be secure. I am the One that should be your focus, not your ministry; so many have fallen because of this error in their thinking."

As I pondered all that had been spoken, I was amazed as I had assumed that swimming in these wonderful waters was going to be my first encounter with God today. I decided to let go of all preconceived ideas of what today would hold, as I had learnt from past experiences *that to assume anything can lead to disappointment. All that God expects of us is to trust Him and to not think ahead or make presumptions of how He will act in our lives.* To truly "let go and let God" was going to be harder than I thought.

As I looked at the waters, I waited for God to encourage me to swim in the depths. After what He had just said, I felt that to edge forward was probably the best option. Little by little I was encouraged forward. The water lapped gently over my ankles and I thought of the many times in church meetings when we had been encouraged to go deeper into God. Water was used as a visual picture to help us understand the Holy Spirit. The water wrapped itself around my knees and I was lifted off my feet. I didn't like this feeling, especially as the reflection of Jesus had long gone off the waters and I felt alone. I had felt this feeling many times in my life when afraid: it felt as if God was not close and I felt lost without His presence.

A voice within said,

"This will always happen when fear takes the place of faith. My children are not meant to fear, I don't reside in fear, only in faith. Step back into faith and you will find Me."

## A LAKE OF DELIGHTS

I could not think of how to convince myself not to be afraid. I then remembered the beginning of my journey. How I had been taught to speak out words of faith; to then see the power of God come through, bringing the truth to release me. I spoke out words of Scripture; at the same time as making sure I believed the truth behind each statement.

"Lord you are my rock and my fortress, in you I trust; you are my shield, my buckler and my very great reward. You will never leave me or forsake me."

As I repeated these words two or three times, being careful to believe them, a change took place in my heart. Strength poured in and loneliness left me. I was annoyed at myself for allowing the feelings to take root without acting sooner. I also realised that *when we have learnt a truth, God expects us to remember it. We can cry out to God for help, but there are many times when God does not answer because He expects us to know the truth. God cannot keep telling us the same truths if we are not prepared to implement them into everyday life.*

I began to relax; floating on my back, feeling completely at ease in the middle of this lake. I rolled around, swishing and swirling, enjoying these wonderful waters, knowing that God was close. I felt a cleansing taking place as I submerged into the depths of the water. I felt no fear as I plunged deeper and deeper. I felt closer to God in the depths than on the surface; *the completeness we find in Him is the treasure of God for each one of us. To be this at ease and secure in Him was a place in which He wanted us all to be.* As I enjoyed this feeling of security, I thought of the many times in my life when everything seemed to be going well; yet I had never felt the security I was feeling now. I had fallen into the hands of the living God; I wanted to remain in this place for the rest of my life.

God's voice echoed across the waters like a steam train across the tracks.

"My child, you are where I want you to be; you are where I want all of My children to be. The difficulty is that I have to test and approve My perfect will for each one of you and until those qualities are tested, you can never know if you have the fullness of the truth of Me within you.

"If you do not have the full truth of Me and My word taking root within your hearts and mind, the enemy can quickly snatch it away, because it is not built on proper foundations. It brings Me great sadness when My children think they suffer over and over again in the same area because I am allowing it, but all I can say is that once they have learnt the truth they will be realised into a greater freedom. My children grow hard in their hearts as they become confused at My ways and they rarely come to Me and ask why they suffer so much, if they did, I could tell them and they would move on quickly. Many of My children think that they are being continually tested and yet they do not understand that if they moved through the tests without resistance, they would reap rewards and have more peace."

I knew the feeling of being frustrated at yet another test; yet I could see that *the reasons we are tried over and over again, is because we do not yield to God in the first place. It is a waste of time resisting God; we have to yield in the end. Can you imagine going to heaven and being shocked at the amount of time you have wasted resisting and not trusting?* After leaving this place, I would return to my normal life and try

## A LAKE OF DELIGHTS

hard to make the most of the truths I was being taught.

As I floated in the waters, I remembered my past and how I had lacked confidence and had not achieved a great deal academically. My lack of confidence left me unable to pursue dreams or ambitions. But here I was, taking part in one of the most amazing experiences anyone could ever imagine and I had not had to gain any major academic achievement to qualify. *The promises of God are there for each one of us. All we have to do is to spend time with Him. God does not want us to struggle to know His truths. Many would find this too easy a concept, as they would rather have a certificate of self-achievement. God provides all that we need for this life and yet many would rather say that they have achieved it all on their own and without God's help. All I can say about my life is that all I have achieved would never have been possible without God's power at work within me. We will never know what we are capable of, unless we yield our lives to Him. As we go to heaven, all that we achieve because of the will of God will go into our eternal history book. It is an amazing feeling to know that when I am obedient to God's will, it will go with me into eternity.*

The fullness of this knowledge was beginning to cause my confidence to grow: as long as I kept on this path, life would be good to me. Even in the difficult times.

A gentle wind started to blow across my face and as the breeze turned into a gale I swam to the shore knowing that for today, this was enough for me to take in and ponder. God wanted the truths He was showing me to take root. As I reached the shore I was surprised to find a man waiting for me. Beside Him was a burning fire, which had overwhelming warmth emanating from it. It was not possible that the type of warmth I felt was only from the fire because it reached into my soul. I sat down to watch the man cooking fish over the fire and my heart was overwhelmed by these wonderful feelings. I asked Him who He was.

"Who do you think I am?" came the reply.

My heart was telling me it was Jesus,

"You are right." He said, "I have waited a long time to be with you in this way. You think that you have longed for this closeness, but not as much as I. Only those who truly seek Me, as you have, will encounter Me in this way. You have longed for My presence throughout your life; valuing My presence above all else. Now sit and enjoy being served."

I sat in awe and I was speechless. The presence that surrounded Jesus was almost visible. I stared in wonder: how could a person carry such presence, peace and joy? *But Jesus is not just any person. He is God!*

I felt such joy that I wondered if I could absorb all that was happening: I didn't want to miss a thing. I felt such a peace, as if I had been drugged; I could hardly speak. If I felt like this on earth there would be no fear, worry, or even slight concern about anything ever again. I wondered how I was going to share this with people when I returned.

Knowing my thoughts, Jesus spoke;

"You know speaking is not a priority when you are full of the Holy Spirit; remember a touch from the King doesn't need any words. One moment in My presence for some people is all they need to change their life forever. My children are more concerned by words than presence. To truly encounter Me would finish intense conversations about who I really am. That is why I say "I Am." No extra words are needed.

## A LAKE OF DELIGHTS

"Many people do not encounter My presence to any degree but there are many ways to find Me. It is life changing for those who have an encounter with Me in a powerful way and it brings them into a relationship with Me in a moment. Unfortunately, for many people this level of My presence is not enough. When they return back to their everyday lives, they rely on their ability to understand what has happened to them and when they have no answers, they quickly fall away.

"My word must be preached, it is all of who I am in words that people can understand, with the power to transform minds and lives. Enjoy this place while you can."

I wanted to feel this way forever. How will I ever explain a feeling and how can I explain to people what I have been experiencing in heaven. Jesus smiled, reached down and touched my brow, with a love that goes beyond words, and as He wiped the tears from my eyes;

He whispered,

"Draw close to Me and I will draw close to you. You will have to work harder at drawing My presence into your everyday life when you return, but you can do it, and as you do, you will affect the lives of those you come across by simply being around them. They will be touched by a little piece of heaven through you."

I knew that we must guard our heart to maintain the presence of God. It would be wonderful to simply walk in His presence without having to be continually filled with His Spirit. But we are in a continuous spiritual battle because of sin in the world. Therefore we must walk closely with God for our own protection from the devil and his schemes. Many Christians struggle setting aside time with God. It is simply a question of choice!

> "Many are the plans in a man's heart,
> but it is the LORD's purpose that prevails."

> Proverbs 19:21

*How will we know the Lord's will, if we don't spend the time with Him? We live in a constant struggle with our fleshly desires pulling us one way while our spirit is trying to guide us to –*

> "...the author and perfecter of our faith..."

> Hebrews 12:2

I felt the joy of being with the Lord begin to overwhelm me again. I thought of so many people that would run into their living rooms every morning if they knew that they could meet with Jesus in this way. *Many people spend more time worrying about how to get a "quiet time" than actually doing it! To spend time with God should be a joy, not a chore. To be soaking in the presence of the Lord; is an all consuming wonderful experience that should be shouted from the roof tops. To be in the presence of the living God and to be swamped with joy and peace should be an expressed emotion of loud praise. Our time with God can be whatever we want it to be, loud, quiet and full of laughter, full of praise, full of His presence, revelation of His word, words of knowledge, prophecy and so many other things. Jesus was opening my eyes to so many possibilities.*

Jesus looked at me with a smile of acknowledgment and said,

"You've got it; that's exactly what you should be thinking! Well, what do you think of the freedom you have?

## A LAKE OF DELIGHTS

Do you like it? All I require is a yielded heart and then I can direct My children's footsteps, moving them in the direction I want them to go for their lives. You will only find true satisfaction when you do this, and yet My children find this so hard. They seem to think that they will miss out and have little or no choice to accomplish all that they want.

"Sadly, many miss out on a wonderful sense of achievement in and through Me. The achievements of man are short-lived and they always come with a price. The achievements of doing My will last an eternity and the joy of being in My will, is ongoing. Eventually, the world will cause you to feel empty, dry and unfulfilled. To have Me as your source will enable you to fulfil your destiny. As I have said before, the soul will only be satisfied with Me as its foundation.

"When you are in My will, you can have a season in which you look as though you are not achieving anything. As far as I am concerned, if it is what you are supposed to be doing, you will be at peace. I will work in the quiet seasons of your life. I could be giving you rest in these times, or doing a deep work in you so that you are ready for the next season. Many of My children fret in these long seasons because they have got so used to bearing fruit. But this is the test all who are Mine must pass. The soul cries out for satisfaction but I should be the One who satisfies your soul. If you cannot exist without each day being filled with activities then you need to make time to get to know the restorer of your soul; the One that is the Bread of Life."

Through these words of wisdom I realised that *God knows the deep recesses of our soul. We cannot expect to change without the restorer of our souls being allowed into every area of our life.* I imagined a life in which we lived so closely to God that we continually exchanged our wisdom for His; living a life of excellence in all we did and thought. *This level of change could only come about if it became part of who we are.* A song burst from the depths of me;

Purify our hearts, Lord, Purify our hearts.
Purify our hearts, Lord purify our hearts.
Be to us a refiner's fire; let us be in the hands of the One who can shape us.
Cause us to be one with You Lord.

It might sound too hard a task; yet how can a heart beat not express itself naturally? When our heart beats with the quickening of the Holy Spirit, we know that God wants to speak to us (or into the lives of those present), through the voice of prophecy. To Bless, encourage, heal and to bind the broken hearted. This is our call and not one of us is exempt.

# Dreams, Faces and Forgiveness

As I looked at the dying embers of the fire, the Lord handed me the food that He had so carefully been preparing. It was such a simple meal and not at all what I was used to. The fish and the chunk of bread, which had been placed at its side, didn't look very appetising. But after one mouthful of the fish, I was pleasantly surprised by its flavour. The bread tasted buttery and soft with a rustic touch. The simplicity of the meal was different to what I was used to, but it was perfect. As I tucked in, I couldn't believe that something so simple brought so much satisfaction. It made me think of the many battles I had in life, when I continually believed that I needed more than what God had provided through His Son. Realising that, the simplicity of knowing Jesus as my source, was enough.

It had been a long day. After the food filled the gap, I felt a deep sleep descend as the swimming took its toll. As I lay down to rest I was asleep before I could thank Jesus for His time and the meal He had cooked. So many thoughts ran through my mind that night; so many dreams and faces appeared: faces of people I hadn't thought about in years. Lots of memories came with the faces, some of them happy, some of them not. Each time a face would appear, a story unfolded of the

## A LITTLE PIECE OF HEAVEN

part they played in my life.

At the end of each story, I found myself standing before God. He asked me if I felt I had played the part He wanted me to in the life of this person. As I thought about this, the ensuing panic that swamped me caused my mind to go blank, as I felt I had played no major part in each of these people's lives. Fear gripped me as I sank to my knees in disbelief.

"I didn't know that you wanted me to do anything for this person." I cried. "You weren't specific."

Out of the midst of the dream, God's voice softly spoke;

"What makes you think that I have asked you to play a major part in any of these lives? All I ask My children to do is to show the fruits of the Spirit to all people. If you rethink, you may find that you did more for these people than you realise. Do not look for the big moments to bless another person or you might miss the gentle encouragement that is needed, or the offer of help. So many times My children are waiting for the bigger gifts to play their part; yet they can continually bless one another by doing what they might regard as small things. In your eyes they are small, but in Mine they are big, because if that is all I have asked of you at that moment, then it is as important as the evangelist preaching to thousands. The size of the task is not as important as the obedience shown."

I woke up startled as I remembered my dream. I realised that I could not recount all of the seemingly small things I had done for people.

I remembered the faces of all the people in the dream. I was pleased to have this opportunity to make sure I

## DREAMS, FACES AND FORGIVENESS

had no grievances with the people in my life. It felt like something you would do at the end of your life and yet here I was in the prime of life being able to set the record straight for eternity. *All of us can do this at any time, but many of us don't. The difference was that I was being shown exactly what I should do in a dream. I wondered why I hadn't done it sooner as God gives us all the ability to forgive and move on.* I was still holding on to things that I thought were minor grievances in the hope they would not be classed as unforgiveness.

Knowing my thoughts, God enlightened me once again;

"The most deceiving mindset a person can have in this area is to think they have forgiven when they haven't. So many of My children say they have forgiven but simply remain hurt by what has happened. Hurt is a relative of unforgiveness; it is a relative that you never get to know, but you always know is there. In other words, you live with the pain but never face it. My children must realise that the hurt that they are expecting Me to heal, can go in an instant. If they come to terms with what it is and begin to pray prayers of blessing on the other person, their hearts will become pure and they will feel a release."

"Oh dear," I thought, "How many times have I waited for God to heal my heart, when it could have been healed in an instant, through a heartfelt prayer of blessing over the person or people that have hurt me?"

I asked God to show me every single person that I had any grievances towards. And He did.

Face after face passed before me and I was overcome with emotion, as I prayed for each one.

## A LITTLE PIECE OF HEAVEN

"Bless them Lord, bless them."

I then stopped as a horrible feeling came over me. I felt as if I was only praying for these people so that God would release me to bless me. Wisdom spoke into my heart; showing me that I simply needed to pray with a pure heart to bless and that I would have known if I had an ulterior motive. I continued to bless and pray for many, even those that didn't pass through my mind. Once I started I couldn't stop—it was infectious. To be able to speak a blessing over people and know that it released the blessing of God on their lives was a wonderful feeling.

After having had many discussions with people who can't seem to forgive, I wondered how I could convey this message in a way that revealed it to their hearts. For some, it would be a stronghold, especially when stubbornness prevented them from forgiving and consequently moving on in their walk with God.

I felt lightness in my heart and joy bubbled up, as the joy took the place of the hurt, which had been there for many years. How could I have been so foolish as to miss out on a blessing because of unforgiveness, when the people that have hurt me are not affected by the hardness in my heart? If only I had understood years ago.

As I lay awake, the night air grew cold and as dew descended on the grass I heard the sound of an owl across the lake. It flew overhead and soared over me in the night sky against a back drop of stars. What a beautiful sight—it took my breath away. I had never seen an owl so close. It was white and its feathers were soft and the loveliest of shades. It came to rest next to me on the rock; I looked into its eyes and got lost in their beauty. This was one of those moments which I rarely had, one of simplicity. It was such a simple thing to do: to sit in silence looking at one of God's creatures. Everything was so still. I rested in the peace of that moment for a long time, thinking of nothing but absorbing the beauty of my surroundings. Life should have been just like this, with no worries or responsibilities.

# The Cave

The next day arrived with a sharp wind blowing: a fine mist covered my face. The sky was black with rain clouds, so I started to look for cover before the clouds burst. As I scanned the lake, I could see a mass of rock on the other side and wondered if I could find cover there. I walked quickly around the lake which had now changed its colour to a midnight blue. The surface transformed from smooth oil like appearance into rough and threatening waters. It's amazing how a change of weather can make you feel different from the night before. As my steps quickened, I noticed a shadow appearing at the side of me and I jumped with fright as I turned around to see who it was.

"Don't worry." a voice said, "I am needed for the next stage of your journey. You'll soon see why."

I couldn't figure out if this person was male or female.

"Who are you?" I said.

The figure replied;

"Don't you remember me from earlier in your journey? You must use your discernment rather than your eyesight. Discernment will give you a much more accurate picture of a person than your eyesight. I was the man you met, just when you needed a little guidance with wisdom, until you found it within you. I am the same person, but in a different form. I know that you have learnt many things since we last met; I am glad to see that your thoughts towards me are beginning to move out of the box. I am needed for the next stage and so here I am."

I steamed ahead as I focused on finding shelter under the rocks. Spots of rain began to hit me with such force that I was glad to see a cave in front of me, which I ran into, closely followed by my guardian. The cave looked dark and damp, yet for some unknown reason it looked familiar. The rock glistened in the dark, as light from outside broke in through a narrow crack above me. The rock looked like coal; in fact the whole cave was covered in it. I had never been in a cave like this before; I was amazed at my surroundings.

I sat down, only to hear the crack of thunder and flashes of lightening breaking through the opening in the rocks above me. The light hit parts of the cave, giving off such a beautiful effect that I sat for ages watching it. To be able to spend time doing something like this brought me peace and a sense of freedom. Previously, my life had been full of so many activities, with little time for things like this, which would have been seen as a waste of time. As I thought about it, I realised that in the world I lived in, there was little time for the simplicity of life, as our value systems had changed so much. Many of these simple pleasures had been lost. But why did this cave look so familiar?

My guide looked at me with knowing eyes;

## THE CAVE

"It's because you have visited this place so many times before."

As I asked him what he meant, he said,

"Most people have been in this cave at some stage in their life. This is where you go when life becomes tough and God seems distant. It is a place of refining and change. This is where you live when going through difficulties; this is where the hidden things are unearthed. That is why coal is on the surface in this cave. In reality coal is excavated from the depths of the earth. Coal is a result of a slow process of many years of plant matter being left to metamorphosize into coal. This process is similar to the hidden emotions in people's lives being left to harden, as more and more unhealed emotions are piled on top. This has to be unearthed for God to complete His work within His people."

I could see from this that even the lightning that broke into this cave was symbolic of God breaking into the dark areas of our lives, highlighting that which needs to be removed.

"Out of the brightness of his presence clouds advanced, with hailstones and bolts of lightning. The LORD thundered from heaven; the voice of the Most High resounded. He shot his arrows and scattered the enemies, great bolts of lightning and routed them."

Psalm 18: 12-14

My guide acknowledged that what I was saying was true. He reassured me that because I had allowed God into these areas many times over the years; allowing healing to take place; that these workings of God would not be as extreme for the rest of my life.

I was pleased to be at a place in my life where the deep workings of God had been done. *Even though, God continues to bring the necessary changes throughout our lives; to enable us to become more like His Son, Jesus.* As I looked at the coal, I could see reflections of people's faces, but I couldn't recognise any of them. They were faces of people that had visited this place over many years. Even though it was not a place I would stay, it was definitely a place all of us must visit to move on in our Christian life. My guide looked at me with such sadness saying,

"You would think that every child of God must have visited this place, but there are many who refuse to pass through for fear of what they might find within themselves. They see others that have visited this place and they have seen the pain that has been unearthed. They have chosen a path in which they are not challenged: one in which their lives remain much the same as when they began their life in Christ."

God's voice echoed around the cave:

"So you see, My child, many do not choose this path. Many would rather look the other way when they see friends who became Christians at the same time as them, changing dramatically. They don't want to know the reasons why they have changed, because deep down they know it's better for them not to know. Everyone has a choice to yield their lives to Me and follow My path for their life. For those that choose to follow Me without restraint, there are many rewards, in this life and the next. But you must follow Me for the right reasons.

"If you are always looking for the rewards at every stage

## THE CAVE

of the journey you will be disappointed, because what you call a reward and what I call a reward can be completely different. The blessings of My kingdom can quite often go unnoticed in a world where financial gain is a priority. Do not look for them; you will see them in time. They remain hidden until the test is passed; then peace comes. Eventually you will see them as you look either at your life or the life of another. But be careful where you look. I change a person's heart in the process of time and they no longer seek after the rewards. Quite often a child of Mine develops strong values of peace and freedom over everything else. Once they have reached this place, they have found what truly matters and I can then bring the abundance of My Kingdom to their lives."

I sighed deeply and wondered at which stage of my journey I was at. *At times it feels as if you are always in some sort of battle and very rarely come to a season of prolonged peace.* I wondered if I could ever reach a long period of calm and quiet in this life. As I looked at my guide, he smiled a knowing smile that spoke a message I already knew into my spirit; *which was that heaven is our home and for now our comfort and peace is found in Jesus.*

The rain had stopped but the thunder and lightning continued to entertain us. It really was a fascinating moment, to find myself in a physical cave that represented a spiritual place in which I had previously spent so much time. It was not a place many would willingly want to revisit but I knew that the rewards within us far outweigh our sufferings. I was enjoying this moment, knowing that God had been answering my questions about life. How strange it was to see the cave with its hidden treasures!

I wondered about all of the people who didn't know Christ and how they coped with spending time in this dark place. My guide spoke with tears in his eyes as he shared his sadness over those that listened to the voice of the enemy in times of difficulty and then became imprisoned by the traps that had been laid in this place. All the traps had been prepared beforehand by the enemy *who knows our weaknesses.*

Suddenly God began to speak through my guide as if He had taken over his body;

"My child, this place is frequented by those that know Me, as well as those that don't. Unfortunately those that belong to Me, quite often listen to the voice of the enemy in times of great stress. Instead of sitting before Me with their Bibles; allowing Me to show them the truth, about their lives and where they are heading because of My promises. Every one of My promises is one hundred percent true for all of My children.

"One of the greatest pitfalls My children make is assuming how and when I am going to come through for them. Disappointment at these times causes many of My children to fall so far that they cannot recover. They hang onto hope but unfortunately their hope is in a particular answer. The only hope My children should have is in the fact that I will never leave them or forsake them. I will make them stronger in the midst of the storm and through every adversity I am working out My purposes. They must praise Me in the midst of difficulties and believe that no matter what they see, I will come through and bring victory. I will do it in My time, in My way and I will achieve My purposes, whether they see it or not. Humility is needed to let go of all reasoning and become like putty in My hands with a humble heart that says, 'Your will be done, your way be done.' When this

## THE CAVE

becomes your portion, when you become completely submitted to Me and My ways then I can truly use you in My Kingdom for great and noble purposes."

I became awestruck at the voice of God speaking through my guide; it was as if God was standing in front of me in person. I was amazed at what I had just heard and how it spoke of the majesty and Kingship of the One I served. I had been frustrated at the ways of God and yet here I was, for the first time, hearing a sound in my spirit, which echoed humility before the King of Kings and the Lord of Lords. Who was I, to ever question God? Yet I did. I thought that because I didn't understand, it gave me a right to ignore or not to believe. How many times have I quietly carried on doing something because I thought I knew better; as I went against the wisdom of God?

I bowed before God in the middle of this cave. I bowed the knee to all of the times I had resisted His will because I didn't understand. I bowed the knee to His ways; in fact, I couldn't stop. I was consumed by His goodness and His grace to me. I began to see that the times I had spent with a hardened heart because of difficult circumstances had been covered by the grace of God. By a God that understood, even when I didn't. I bowed and bowed in this cave of darkness. This was the place where I had learnt about God and His ways. If I hadn't spent so much time in this place, with so many questions and so much soul searching, I wouldn't know God in the way that I did.

This place looked beautiful and majestic. The coal glistened and as I looked more closely I saw something else locked up inside the coal. I moved closer and as I did, all I could see were clusters of tiny diamonds embedded in the rock. Thousands upon thousands of them appeared as the light continued to break in. As the storm clouds passed and the light increased, they sparked off rays of light in all directions.

"I can see my face, in the diamonds." I shouted, "I can see my face."

I fell to my knees as I realised that God was showing me the times in my life when each difficulty I had gone through, produced a diamond in my character. Here I was, seeing them in the natural. Each one was chiselled perfectly for a purpose and was shaped for a specific tool in the lives of others. I was amazed as I saw that they were formed at the worst times in my life. I now understood what God meant when He said that the rewards He gives us, sometimes, come in different forms to what we expect. Some of these rewards were eternal rewards because the character changes that take place within, enable us to be a blessing in the lives of others as we become more Christ like. There were rewards for now as well as the future, as we affected people and brought them to a place of victory. It would go down in the eternal history book of my life, as well as for all of those who visited this place and chose to go through this refining process.

I loved being in the cave and I loved all that God was showing me, but I felt compelled to move on. My guide beckoned me to the entrance of the cave and as I walked forward, I was determined to remember my time here, so that I could share with others who also decide to walk with God in the way that I had. As I stepped out of the cave and looked at the lake I was aware that it possessed a tranquillity that reminded me of the calm after the storm. For me, this symbolised the feelings of peace

## THE CAVE

I used to have after coming through one of the many trials I encountered in the early days of my Christianity. I needed to rest and ponder over the day's events. I was so glad I had begun this journey, even though there were many times since becoming a Christian I had thought otherwise. My knowledge of God and His wonderful love for His children was increasing and I loved every minute of understanding the grace that was mine.

# Dancing with the King

I was beginning to feel as if I was a completely different person; I saw life differently and I saw people in a different light. I wondered how I had not seen as clearly as this before. *This life is so short and the desires of our heart are so temporal. If only we could live each day being more aware of our eternal destiny, I am sure we would behave differently towards one another. If only we could accept that every action was seen in the light of eternity; unfortunately all of us seem so earth focused. So much time wasted; fretting and worrying about this life and all of its problems with longings for more fulfilment. All we need is found in Jesus. Our contentment in this life is found in Him; we just need to believe it and seek Him with all of our heart.* This is the first commandment:

"Love the LORD your God with all your heart and with all your soul and with all your strength."

Deuteronomy 6:5

As I thought about this, God spoke to me again and reminded me of the Israelites in the desert, who were being fed the same food every day. They decided that it was not enough as they remembered the variety of food they had eaten in Egypt. They thought they knew better

# A LITTLE PIECE OF HEAVEN

and that God was withholding the best from them.

God's voice echoed around me;

"You must believe that whatever you are given, at each stage of your life, is enough. Your life is not about quality or quantity, it is about Me. It has and always will be about Me. What you desire will never replace what I can give you. Do not sacrifice this knowledge in the hope of getting something better."

I sank to my knees with the knowledge of the biggest deception the world has ever known. *The biggest stumbling block to mankind is to believe that we can have more than what we already possess in Jesus Christ. Even if we have nothing as far as the world is concerned, we have everything in Him.*

As I continued to walk alongside the lake, God's peace surrounded me. All I wanted to do was to walk in His presence and see His creation. As the waves lapped over the shore the peace of God soaked the atmosphere and with every step I became addicted to feeling this way — was I dreaming? *How could we want anything else in this life?* I started to worship, and my voice sang out to the King of Kings, songs that I had never heard, with a voice I didn't know I possessed. From the depths of me, the words that came were truth and life. These words were unearthed from my knowledge of God and they flowed from me like a river as I entered a new heavenly realm.

Suddenly the scenery around me transformed. Angels appeared from nowhere, surrounded by an array of lights. Lights which contained colours I had never seen; colours that spoke of majesty; colours which spoke of the beauty of the Lord, whilst there were others that spoke of the suffering of the saints for the sake of the Gospel. They were vibrant, rich and deep. They surrounded the throne room of God and they symbolised the sacrifice of many. There were colours that were delicate: these were symbolic of the children that had been taken and gently lifted into the heavenly realms and surrounded the heart of God. Then there were colours that were soft and gentle; those were in the hands of God and symbolised the prayers of the most humble of His saints. These saints didn't look for fame or recognition but were happy to pray for those in need and to help those God brought to them.

As I looked at the colours as a whole, they complemented each other and formed a mosaic, in which I could see the face of Jesus. The angels danced amongst the colours, rejoicing in their beauty with the knowledge that the people they represented would be here one day, seeing all of this beauty; knowing that not one tear would pass unnoticed. Some were dancing wildly with such passion and as they danced they interceded for the saints. The passion with which they danced took my breath away, as I had never seen anyone care so much about one individual, as these angels did for the whole of mankind. Some were warrior angels, while others were intercessory angels, who all danced together with one heart, fighting in the spirit for those that desperately needed help.

All of a sudden light broke forth and a flash of lighting signalled the end of the intercession. There was a spiritual breakthrough which immediately affected the lives of those who had been targeted in prayer.

A group of angels appeared clothed in white, pure white. They slowly walked up to the throne room of God as they danced and bowed. It was such a beautiful sight as they praised God with pure and thankful hearts for the sacrifice His Son had made. I wondered why the worship in our churches didn't touch this and I hoped that one day it would. The whole place began to erupt in loud praise as they danced. People appeared from everywhere including saints from generations past. They were leaping and dancing with no inhibitions. Now this was what I called praise! The joy that was on the faces of these saints was expressed with such vibrancy; I couldn't believe what I was seeing. This is what I will enjoy for eternity with many loved ones. I will be able to dance with them forever in this place. Oh how I longed for the world to experience what I was now seeing and feeling! I couldn't help but dance; it was so wonderful and so thrilling. To be able to dance freely without thinking about it; all to the joy of the Lord!

A bubbling of joy arose from the depths of me and my dancing became wilder and more passionate. I weaved my way through the angelic beings, through the colours and the saints. I smiled like I had never smiled before and I squealed with delight as the joy overtook me. I was overwhelmed with such energy and I was able to dance in front of Jesus as He sat on His throne. And then to my amazement, He joined me and He held my hands as we ran through the sea of faces, swirling around and around. It was amazing to be able to dance with Jesus; holding His hands, with such love flowing between us; such beauty to behold.

As the music slowed down, I fell into the arms of Jesus. He lowered me down and sat at my side propping me up. As His arm fell around my shoulders, I could hear His heart beat. I was taken aback as each beat of His heart spoke of His passion for the people He had been sent to save. I longed to feel this passionate for His people and yet I couldn't manufacture what I was now experiencing.

Jesus looked at me and smiled;

"Walk closely with Me and My heart beat will become yours. This is all I ask of you: draw close to Me at every moment of every day and My heart for people will become yours."

I felt the scene fading. As I looked up, I could see that I had returned to the side of the lake. I longed to return to my previous heavenly encounter where such goodness and love surrounded me. There were no more colours and the dancing had gone. How could I be happy with anything else after that?

A voice within said;

"Don't forget that I have given you the ability to be content in all circumstances. Remember what you have just learnt; I am everywhere and you have the ability to feel My presence, just like Paul did, while he was in prison."

I knew that God would have to test me over many years, before this became part of my foundation. The important thing was that I *believed* it was possible to move into a place of complete surrender to this truth. It would be more than I could bear to have tasted the best, only to have it taken away.

*Feelings of joy and peace cannot be our goal; they are the icing on the top of the cake.* As I bowed my head in humility, I prayed and sought the face of Jesus before I went to sleep.

"Lord, whether I feel Your presence or not, I know that You are here and that You live within me. I stand in faith to know that I am in Christ and that You live in me by

## A LITTLE PIECE OF HEAVEN

Your Holy Spirit. Nothing will rob me of this truth, I am Yours and You are mine, thank you Lord."

Warmth entered my soul. I lay down and as my eyes closed, I remembered the angels dancing and the wonderful colours that I had seen that day.

# Mending the Nets

I awoke the next morning to the clash of cymbals and the blast of trumpets. I grabbed my jumper, stood to my feet and ran to the water's edge to see a boat on the water. The water looked so calm and yet the noise of the instruments shattered the quietness.

"Come on." a voice shouted, "Over here."

As I turned around, a lady appeared at my side and ushered me forward.

"We are going to watch the King fish."

This did not seem as though it would be an enthralling thing to watch from a distance, but at the lady's command, I ran to the water's edge. The lady was gaunt and her clothes were ragged and dirty; her hair was long and straggly. I was taught not to judge by appearances but I couldn't believe anyone would turn up to greet a King looking like this.

We stood looking out over the lake. I saw the boat getting nearer; a net hung over the side. The boat drew as close as it could to where we were standing and I could just about see Jesus repairing the nets. They were old and ripped; I could not see how anyone could catch fish with a net like that.

## A LITTLE PIECE OF HEAVEN

As I looked up, I saw Jesus smile at me;

"You will be surprised at the fish you can catch with broken nets. My people are constantly catching fish with broken nets. You see, My church is a broken net and the people in it look as poor and broken as the lady standing next to you. You wouldn't think so by their outward appearances, but if you could see what I can see, you will see a people that look as spiritually poor and torn on the inside as the lady standing next to you looks on the outside. Many cannot see the condition of My bride as you can now, but this is the truth."

As I looked at the lady standing next to me, she looked nothing like a bride. I was saddened that we looked like this to God, as His children and His bride. *How foolish we are to think we can pretend to be all that we are supposed to be by turning up at church week after week. Hiding what Jesus sees all the time.* I had never seen the church like this, but I could not see the condition of our souls.

Jesus looked at me with a surprised expression and said,

"Didn't you know My church looks like this? I love her anyway; I always have and always will, but I long for My bride to be spotless. My Father sees My righteousness when He looks at His children, but I have to see the condition of each soul so that I can do my work. I am under no illusions as to the condition of My people. My sadness is that *they* are under illusions. Many see themselves in a different light; this is My great sadness. When they see themselves as they really are; only then can they begin to change. The net that you see here is broken and yet I am able to catch fish. This is symbolic of the church and its current state. For the church to be more effective it must repair its broken nets. Sin always finds its way in when My people are not wholly following Me.

"You found it difficult coming to the water's edge with the lady I sent to get you because she looked like a tramp. And yet you worship in church every week with people whose souls are in a worse condition than this lady's outward appearance."

I cried out, "But what can I do about the state of other people's souls? I can only try my best to be all that *I* can be, with the help of the Holy Spirit."

Jesus raised His voice;

"Cry out for My people: they are like lost sheep. They think that those that have gone astray are the back sliders, but I would describe lost sheep as those who are poor and wretched on the inside, whether they are in or out of church. My people think that they can hide behind the facade of church, but I see all and I know all and I am not pleased with the standards I see in the church today. Purity is not preached and purity is not seen. My people are led astray by false doctrines and false prophets, who come to preach words that are not Mine. The lady that came to bring you here today began the day with a clashing of symbols and a sounding of the trumpets. You were caught off guard; it was not the sort of praise that you would have enjoyed in a church meeting and she was not the sort of person you would have wanted standing next to you on a Sunday morning. But I tell you that this lady has a pure, humble heart and she represents many that worship Me. Their singing and praise is not so refined but it comes from a heart that overflows with true love for Me and My ways.

## A LITTLE PIECE OF HEAVEN

"What you hear in today's churches is a poor representation of true praise because true praise must be in spirit and truth; flowing out of a pure heart from those who are in relationship with Me. You see My child, I always look at what is going on within My children and I only hear those that worship Me in spirit and truth. I do not care for any other type of worship; no matter how wonderful it may sound to you.

"Where two or three are gathered in My name to worship and praise Me with pure hearts; their worship is sweet; it ministers to Me more than any other type of worship.

"If you desire to touch heaven with your worship, you must only gather with those that worship Me in spirit and truth. Then you will truly enter heaven on earth. This type of worship reaps spiritual rewards and is more satisfying than hours of worship full of technical excellence but lacking any true expression of love to God our Father.

"When you return, you must only go where I tell you to go to worship. Do not measure a person or a place by what appears to be success. I will guide you to where you will be blessed by the people and by the praise. My people have stopped saying, 'God is here.' People have started singing the praises of the voices of those that sing and the beauty of the songs. They no longer want to encounter Me. They want to encounter a level of Me in the songs but the perfection and the presentation of the songs has become more important. The eloquence of the words is more important than their meaning. When My Holy Spirit directs a meeting it can appear messy and disorderly, but I can assure you that there will be a Godly order that cannot be fathomed by man. Man has lost trust in My ability to organise. Some of My churches have become polished vessels, but it is not My polish and not My vessel, it is theirs!

Jesus passion filled the atmosphere as He continued to speak;

"My order must be returned to the church; My presence must be valued above all else. Do people want to be attracted to the church or to Me? The church has become a vessel that functions for its own purpose and for its own glory instead of Mine. They value numbers of people, where many gather to worship Me, but very few are true worshippers. My leaders must question the values of the church and they must seek My face again for what is truly of value to Me and My Kingdom. They must return to being reliant on Me and only Me.

"To preach from a pulpit on a Sunday is a very responsible role and yet My ministers have created their own pulpits with their own messages. Woe to those that preach words other than the words that will feed My sheep! Each minister is accountable to Me for the words that leave their mouths. Many of My children have walked away or fallen on account of careless words. It is time for the true shepherds to arise and feed My sheep. My sheep who are starving and stunted in their growth.

"My bride is in a bad condition because of this."

As I looked at the face of Jesus, He continued to mend the nets. I could see that His heart was not to condemn, but to build up and mend the damage that had already been done. His love for the church is endless and His heart cries out for those that would rise up and take their rightful place and speak His words of truth. *God is looking for those that look to Him for increase in their congregations. Numbers are not a gauge for success; as long as they are obedient; even in the midst of criticism, they will receive the blessings for their obedience.*

Jesus looked at me and smiled a smile that lifted my spirit. He knew I was sad and that I felt a concern for the people of God. I wondered where the church was going and how we can be deceived by a false measure of success. I wasn't sure where we went from here and how the churches that Jesus spoke of could correct their errors. It seemed too big a task for those that had already committed themselves to build a church under a certain style or ethos. My next thought surprised me as I began to feel that it was better to be a door keeper in the house of the Lord than to be responsible for taking the church in the wrong direction.

Jesus replied;

"Ahh, wise thought. There is only one problem with it. Every person has a call on their life to fulfil their destiny. So if you are called to preach, then to be a doorkeeper is as bad as taking the church in the wrong direction. To truly follow Me you need to be humble and to be cleansed of ambition. Those that have truly allowed Me into their lives regardless of success are those that will always be on the right path. The danger comes when people think that they are successful because of their own achievements. They can then begin to wander into fleshly ideas and plans.

"All you need to do is to allow Me to be the anchor of your soul. I am the One that pulls you into harbour when you are beginning to drift. To do this you need to remain in the waters of the Holy Spirit."

## MENDING THE NETS

I sat down and watched Jesus as He continued to mend the nets. There was no pulling or tugging at the bits that He needed to get rid of; they were already hanging on by a thread. As He washed the mended nets and lifted them out of the water, they looked brand new. He threw them to one side and concentrated on the torn and ragged ones; I could see that His attention was no longer needed on the mended nets. Jesus would not stop mending the nets until they were as He wanted them to be, to enable them to catch all of the fish.

It was midday and as Jesus came ashore, it was time to serve Him. What a privilege! What was I going to prepare for lunch and how would I best serve Jesus? It was such a big task, that I didn't know where to start. My eyes suddenly caught sight of the lady that had been patiently waiting for this moment to arrive and she beckoned me to sit and watch. As I sat down next to a rock I melted into my surroundings and felt that I was just about to enjoy something unique.

The shadow that had fallen on me as the midday sun descended caused me to be shielded from the heat. As peace surrounded me, I looked up to see the lady bathing the Lord's feet as He stepped onto the shore. She dried His feet with her long straggly hair. I felt quite indignant by this scene; in my eyes Jesus deserved more than dirty, straggly hair to dry His feet. But the Lord was not interested in outward appearances. He was ministered to by the heart of the lady that served Him. Her gentleness was evident as she carefully cared for each foot, meticulously drying every part. As she took her time, it was obvious she didn't want her time serving Jesus to end. Serving people had not been this enjoyable in my own life: I would normally do it quickly, like any other task.

I noticed a tear rolling down the lady's cheek, as the

love she felt for her Master overwhelmed her. Each foot was placed carefully back on dry ground and she beckoned Jesus towards the fire, where she had been cooking all morning. She was so focused on serving her Master. To love and cherish someone this much, would naturally cause you to get up early, simply for the privilege of serving. I then realised that I would have to go a long way to have such a pure and simple heart, towards God and the life He had for me. We sat together around the fire and enjoyed — yet more fish!

Jesus looked up to speak to me as He knew that I was dissatisfied with the same food.

"Remember what I told you earlier when the Israelites were dissatisfied with the same food. Always remember that your focus is Me and that I am the One that feeds your soul; I am the Bread of life."

We ate, talked and laughed together for the rest of the afternoon. There were times when I simply couldn't believe that this was happening to me. To relax in His presence as I was doing now was the best fellowship. I was learning more by talking to Jesus than through any Bible study I had ever done. I remembered the Scriptures and the time Jesus spent with His disciples; it must have been so precious. I loved being in His presence and as the hours passed I didn't want it to end. As Jesus bid us goodbye, we watched Him get back into the boat to carry on mending the nets. He was not fretful of the enormity of the task or concerned about time. He simply knew the times and the seasons for all that He did.

I fell asleep that night wondering how I would know the times and the seasons for my own life. As the sun went down and the last rays of sunshine disappeared, I remembered how secure I had felt when I sat with Jesus. My life was completely in His hands. All I needed to do was to surrender to His will. I fell into a deep sleep and as I slept, my dreams took the place of the peace that I had felt earlier in the day. I dreamt of the pain of losing someone I loved and the fear of it happening again which then caused me to toss and turn. After experiencing my own great loss the thought of grieving for a long period of time, after coming through the healing process was just too much. The dream was convincing me that I was going to have to go through many years of grief as I lost the older generation of my family. The faces of the people that I was going to lose at some stage of my life appeared in front of me and the trauma and loss was overwhelming.

I awoke to find my face was wet with tears. As I looked into the star lit sky, I remembered the promises that God had given to Abraham and the blessings that came with them. The stars were scattered across the night sky; I knew that this was a sign for me to believe that, no matter what, God had covered my life with His grace and promises. For every situation I had to go through, He had gone before me. My fears subsided as my thoughts exposed that I needed to trust in the Maker of heaven and earth. As I looked up, I felt a peace come over me again which spoke of my future. That one day I would be complete in Him and that there would be no more tears and no more pain. God was weaving His purposes into His people and even into creation and here I was looking at the wonder of the night sky. As the moon shone it gave off such a bright light that the stones around me glistened like diamonds. I drifted off to sleep feeling utterly secure in Him.

# A Very Special Occasion

"Come on!" a voice shouted, "You will miss it, if you don't get up now." "Miss what?" I replied. "Come on!" the lady shouted.

I jumped up and ran with a sense of urgency in my spirit. I looked at the lady in front of me and I was astounded by her beauty; her clothes were amazing. I ran and tried to catch up with her. As I glanced over, I could see that her face was radiant and bright. Her hair flowed down her back and it was the most beautiful colour I had ever seen; chestnut brown with strong shades of gold and red. I couldn't believe that this was the lady I had seen yesterday: she looked like a completely different person.

"What has happened to you?" I shouted.

She smiled and encouraged me to run faster, saying,

"We need to be on time, you don't want to miss anything!"

I ran along the lakeside, until we came to an abrupt stop next to some large trees. As I looked beyond the trees, I was astounded. There were so many people: singing and dancing with cymbals clashing and drums beating. Each was singing a different song and yet it was beautiful. They were celebrating and I just had to join them.

## A LITTLE PIECE OF HEAVEN

"Worthy, worthy, worthy." they sang.

I ran straight into the middle of the crowd. It felt like a Caribbean festival that was full of colour, with all sorts of musical instruments. Brightly coloured streamers were being thrown in the air; balloons were floating past: there were colours, so many colours. They were the colours of celebration; colours of joy, such joy! The people spun around each other whilst dancing to celebrate the saints that had just arrived and had received the crown of life. They danced as they celebrated past and present saints. It was as if they were crowning the King of glory with their songs. There was such a sense of the majesty of God in the atmosphere. I had never encountered this type of freedom when dancing with people on earth, it was truly liberating. We danced around the lake over and over again and as the lake became brighter I could see a golden glow, hovering just above it. The lake was full of life and as we praised, the life in it grew. *Oh, how I wish we knew this as we worshipped in our church meetings! Worship brings Him alive on the inside of us.* The life of God was evident in each believer as they danced.

Out of nowhere a shower of angels appeared blowing trumpets and swooping down across the heads of those worshipping; it was a glorious sight to behold. I then saw a group of people appearing and they were the Jews, the chosen race. The heartbeat of God was amongst these people as they danced and sang,

> "Adonai, Adonai, praise our God
> in heaven most high!"

The music echoed in my heart. The heartbeat of God was evident through the Jewish people, even though I had never seen them as being any different to the rest of

## A VERY SPECIAL OCCASION

His children. God was now revealing that they were a special people; those that would usher in the very presence of the King in the last days. They were the entrance by which He would return. *But before that happens, they must become the people that God has ordained them to be.* I remembered the Scripture that spoke of praying for the peace of Jerusalem; these people must to be ready! It was as if they were the red carpet that would welcome Jesus back to claim His inheritance.

A sea of voices began to worship God in complete harmony. I sat in wonder absorbing the effect of these worshippers as they lavished their love upon God. As they sang, I could see something rising from the hearts of the people; the spirit of God began to reveal to me that they were weights which the saints had carried for some time. They were the responsibilities they had carried all of their lives; it was the call of God on each life. Some carried them as a personal burden and others had learnt to keep their burdens light as God had ordained them to be.

"For *my* yoke is easy and *my* burden is light."

### Mathew 11:30

With each release, I could sense a lightness enter the hearts of these new saints as they realised they had arrived at the place where there were no more burdens. Joy broke out on their faces as the burdens left them. So many sighs were heard as they received the joy of the Lord. Then another sound was heard. This time, it was the saints and they were singing a new song. It was a song of praise for all that God had accomplished through their lives. The praise kept on coming as their eyes were opened to all that God had done for them, including His protection over their lives and the many times He brought the wisdom that stopped them making wrong decisions.

The saints started to cry and weep, at the same time as singing, but they were tears of joy. They exchanged their ashes for beauty. Their tears dried up as the Holy Spirit opened their eyes to past victories that arrived just when they were ready to give up. They saw how their heart and flesh would have failed them, if Jesus had not strengthened them and given them what they needed, just in time. The singing became louder, as God revealed all that each saint had accomplished in and through Him. I was so moved by this scene that I could not stand; I was overwhelmed with the emotion of the moment as I had never seen such gratitude expressed in singing. The depths of feeling were beyond words as the beauty of each song was heard by all. Many of the saints lay on the floor in silence, unable to speak for hours, while others continued to sing.

As this scene became imprinted on my mind, I sat and remembered the cross and all that it had accomplished. I could see that *the smallest act of obedience is nothing, in comparison to what Jesus has done for us. And yet to be disobedient in the smallest of things, shows that we don't understand the cross and the power of obedience.* How many times have I turned away from what I know I should do? After seeing this scene and realising that *the smallest act of obedience will be remembered and shown for what we have accomplished in God*, I decided to make every effort to have an eternal view of my life on returning to earth.

The lady that had brought me to this place appeared at my side and reminded me not to dwell on past failures, but to rejoice in my new future in God; a future in which I would be able to walk the path He had set before me.

## A VERY SPECIAL OCCASION

As the music died, the rejoicing turned to a quiet contemplation. I was surprised by the peace that entered the atmosphere. With the stillness came a descending mist and as I sat and watched the mist settle, an overwhelming peace entered my heart, stilling all of my thoughts. I watched the mist cover all who were in this place as God's glory came down in a form that seemed almost human as it wrapped itself around the people. The form twisted, turned and stretched as if it was dancing: it touched each person as it passed, including the angels. As it touched each person they became overwhelmed with wonderful emotions. There were tears, laughter and at times, screams of delight for some as the Spirit of God surrounded them completely.

I wondered what would happen when I encountered the Spirit of God, but before I could think any more the Holy Spirit was upon me and I fell to my knees. I had longed for an experience like this and here I was being swamped by the Holy Spirit, with no more restrictions. It was as if I had all the time in the world to encounter the Holy One, I became like a sponge in His presence, ready to absorb all of who He was. I felt as if I was being changed into His image with all of my impurities melting away. I could not retain my thoughts; only those thoughts that were His. All of God's thoughts towards me kept entering my mind and I felt His overwhelming love towards me. I recalled times of doubt in my life, as God showed me what I should have thought in those times. I sobbed tears of joy, as I realised how foolish I had been to ever doubt His love in the hard times. Ongoing revelations of how God had helped me throughout my life were coming to me. *When we see our life through His eyes, strongholds in our thinking can be broken and we can be truly effective.* I felt regret at the times I had not let go of my train of thought and taken the necessary steps of faith to move forward, regardless of circumstances, into a place of peace and trust. So much emotion had been wasted at these times, so much wasted time instead of trusting and moving on in Him.

The regret I felt, quickly disappeared, in the midst of being soaked in the Holy Spirit. I had never felt so clean and renewed in my mind, with much of my old way of thinking being removed and the revelation of God taking its place. I saw God in a new way as my eyes were opened to more of His truths. As I stood up and looked around, I saw that everyone else was having the same experience. I felt honoured to be amongst all of these people who seemed to be more worthy than I of this privilege.

The lady looked at me and asked;

"Why do you think you are any less special than they are? You are all God's children?"

"Because they look radiant and pure and I don't look the same." I replied.

The lady placed a mirror in front of me and I was overwhelmed by the beauty I could see; my face shone with the glory of the Lord. I could see the same purity in me as I could in them. I couldn't believe the new me looked so wonderful, with Jesus shining out of me.

The lady looked at me and smiled;

"All of God's children are blessed in the same way. Why should you be any different from them?"

Suddenly, autumn leaves began to fall all around me; the colours were so beautiful: gold, red, and orange. The leaves were dying and yet they were beautiful, how

## A VERY SPECIAL OCCASION

could that be? How can death appear to be so beautiful? I then realised that *the right sort of dying is beautiful. A dying of self in the season ordained by God is always beautiful.* This is what the leaves were symbolising. I remembered the times that I had gone through difficulties and I couldn't understand the purposes of God. But when I looked back and remembered how I used to behave. I could see that part of me had died in those times and that a deposit of Godly character was put in its place. *So this is what God sees when we are going through tough times; He sees the beauty of the death rather than the pain of dying. He sees new birth, maturity and a new season in which we can display more of His glory.*

# Higher Up the Mountain

As I looked up and revelled in all that I saw, I realised that the falling leaves were symbolising a new season and a new day for me and I was going higher up the mountain of the Lord. Everything had been so beautiful by the lake, which made it harder to move on. As I looked up, I waved goodbye to all of the saints that had come into this wonderful place and received the crown of life. They continued to rejoice and delight in their inheritance; it was glorious to behold and joy burst into my heart at seeing the blessing of the saints in glory. I could not help but yearn to be with them. It tore at the very core of me to know that I must return to the world at some stage, as this place was beyond my imagination and desires. To have these inexpressible emotions caused my heart to ache with the pain of leaving.

God spoke:

"I know that leaving here is hard, but you don't know what the next stage of your journey holds. I can assure you, that if you trust Me and give Me your emotions, I will make sure you are able to let go of this yearning. You will have a natural desire to move on. I have put destiny on the inside of you and your purpose will compel you forward."

## A LITTLE PIECE OF HEAVEN

As God's words left their mark upon my soul, I cried out and asked God to release me from these feelings, to enable me to move on. As I did this, a cloud descended and everything faded from view. My emotions calmed as I walked ahead into all that God had for me. As I walked, I looked back and saw the lake that I had spent so much time around. The cave appeared small and the place where I had sat and been served by Jesus disappeared in the cloud. God had more to show me and if I had not moved forward, I would have missed out on so much. The mountain air was refreshing and caused me to feel more awake than the air around the lake, which had been warm and comfortable. The whole area around the lake spoke of comfort. I remembered the way in which I was waited on by Jesus and the guide who continually appeared every time I needed wisdom; until I found wisdom within. The ease of that place caused me to rest in its comfort and I realised that to fulfil my destiny, I could not have remained. I had grown in my understanding of God and His ways and I realised that this was preparation for the next stage. *It can be too easy for us to remain in a place of comfort in the world that we live, just like I had done here. But God calls us all to fulfil our destiny and to keep moving forward. We must remember that we are moving through our destiny not only towards it, as we touch the lives of those we meet and in turn other people touch ours.*

The air became fresher as I climbed the mountain. I turned around one more time to remember the lake and as I did, an eagle soared in front of me and blocked my view. I tried to look at the lake and remember, but all I could see was the eagle soaring beautifully. It was impossible not to watch, as it caught the air pockets, using them to climb higher and higher. As it got closer, I could see the mass of feathers that covered its body.

## HIGHER UP THE MOUNTAIN

What a magnificent sight!

I then realised that the eagle was purposefully getting in my way; it did not want me to take one last look. As the eagle soared he circled me, over and over again, until he was above my head, causing me to look up at him. I felt wisdom speak into my spirit to tell me that the next stage was a higher place in God: one in which the experiences of the lake needed to be forgotten, to enable me to enjoy where I was now. I must look to God and know that there were better things to come.

As the eagle flew away, a peace entered my heart and I heard the wisdom of the Holy One within telling me to rest. I was not sure where to rest, but as I climbed higher I could see a place tucked out of the way in the cleft of the rock. As I sat under the rock, a shadow covered me. But it was no ordinary shadow. I could feel the presence of God in it; I was not alone and the comfort I felt as I slumped into the rock was wonderful. It was somewhat different up here, than below by the lake. After being surrounded by God's love through His people, I battled with feelings of loneliness. I liked the feel of the constant companionship; in comparison the mountain seemed quiet and still.

And yet the presence of God was stronger and His voice clearer:

"I am your soul food whether it is loneliness or any other emotion; I am a constant source of provision for every area of your life. The higher up the mountain you go, the lonelier the walk. The lake is where many of the saints reside and where the most visible activity is seen. It is a place of comfort, where many of My people rest in their faith. And yet I have called you to climb higher. It is not that you are superior to other people, it is simply your calling and it is a difficult one. Those who are not climbing the heights will not understand your walk. You will even find that you begin to speak a different language to those with whom you used to identify. Remaining in My presence will become more important as you move higher up the mountain. My ways become higher and more difficult for you to understand as the working of My Spirit takes you on paths that cannot be fathomed by man. And so a greater level of trust is required. You will understand My ways in time and you will need to exercise more faith, as well as more courage.

"The heights to which I take you will cause you to shudder with fear at times. You will see how far you have come and you will realise that you simply cannot go back to the way things were. You will have taken steps of faith away from the world and all of its ways. To return with the knowledge you have gained would be burdensome. Doubt is your enemy; it becomes an even greater enemy to you as you climb. You cannot afford to weaken in your resolve as you climb the mountain, else the enemy will pick you out and destroy your ability to believe. But if you do fall, the only way back is to believe again and to speak out words of faith, in the same way you did at the beginning of your journey.

"The emotional beating you take when you fall can sometimes be too much for those closest to you. They see you lose heart as you share your doubts and fears with them, but they are not on the same walk as you. Their voices of doubt and negativity will reinforce all that you fear, because lack of understanding produces negativity. No-one will understand or believe your unique walk, so you need to walk very closely with Me. Trust Me and allow Me to be your guide; even if you fail to hear Me correctly,

# HIGHER UP THE MOUNTAIN

I will find a way to put you back on track. You have come a long way already, My child, but you have to realise that the walk you are on is not about you. It is about those I am sending you to, so that you can help them on their journey through life. You have a call to restore what is broken My child."

I absorbed all that God spoke to me and as the last of the sun dipped behind the horizon, I thanked the Lord for all of His encouragement and curled up in the warmth of the rock and went to sleep.

I awoke the next morning, to feel hailstones hitting the rock above me. A cold chill surrounded me, so I decided to run up the mountain, asking God to direct me to better shelter. This place was remote and unwelcoming. As my steps quickened, I looked up and saw the sun shining at the top of the mound I was climbing and I was beckoned forward by the warm glow. As the ground warmed in front of me, it melted the hailstones; as well as melting my fears of being left in a place that was remote and lonely. The sun was bright and I ran as fast as I could to get away from the stagnant feel of the cleft of the rock. To move forward was far better than to remain in a place of stagnation. The freshness of the place I now found myself in caused my soul to shout praises to God. I was beginning to move on, by my own choice and it felt good.

I was on a journey to know God in a deeper way and as I got to the top of the mound, I saw a figure in the distance.

It was Jesus! He had a golden glow around Him. Something had changed and as I caught up with Him, He felt more like a close friend. What a delight! I wasn't sure if I would see Him for some time and I was beginning to miss the fellowship I had enjoyed by the lake. As I caught up with Him, He was delighted to see me and His arm came around my shoulder as He drew me close to His side and said,

"This is what you can expect from now on. To have Me at your side and to be this close is the reward for those that follow Me up the mountain. Even though this walk is not about your focus on rewards, your choice naturally comes with many blessings. Your heart has to be pure to follow Me in this way. If rewards are your goal you are likely to turn back when life gets tough and rewards are few. You have chosen well, My child. Well done! I have much to show you, let's walk and enjoy the sunshine and the day. I want you to enjoy My presence in this place."

I walked and talked with Jesus for many hours, enjoying the wonderful scenery as we walked up the mountain. There were times when I looked at the Lord and His face was so full of emotion, as we talked about His desire for God's people to know Him more. He told me about the sacrifice of our earthly lives, in exchange for a deeper knowledge of Him and His ways. He told me how many desired to know the Lord more and yet many refused to give up activities that took them further away from God. It was disappointing to hear of many that refused this path because of the call of the world and the draw of what was familiar and secure. One of the biggest sacrifices for most people was to walk a path on which those closest to them were not on. They knew it would bring relationship challenges; ultimately leading to losing closeness with those they had once enjoyed strong bonds.

I remembered the times I had to let go of conversations

that once stimulated my social times; my mind was renewed as a result and I started to disagree with those I used to be in agreement with. It was a difficult thing to do, but *when you know you are being taught in line with the truths of God, you cannot turn back.*

Jesus told me about many that walked this journey for a while, until the cost became too great and then without looking back, turned away and got lost in all that the world had to offer. They chose the world instead of forsaking the short-lived rewards of this life; missing out on the rich fruit of Kingdom living and our eternal rewards. He also told me about those who turned back just before they were about to break through into a better place and reap the rewards of holding on to Him and His plan for them. This was His great sadness.

There were many that had been steadfast in their walk, only to lose out on all that was stored up for them in their breakthrough season. The pain on the face of Jesus, as He relayed these stories, was more powerful than words. I remembered times, when I felt the same overwhelming urge to give up, but thankfully I drew closer to Jesus in the difficult times, rather than pushing Him away. And yet, I saw how easy it would have been for me to walk away.

*We cannot persuade those that fall away to return and we cannot convince those that are struggling to remain steadfast. It is a personal choice to walk with God or walk away from God. The only thing we can ever do is pray and hope people make the right choice.*

As we walked, the Lord spoke to me about all of those that had struggled the most and had nearly decided to give up on many occasions, but then at the last moment decided to push through into victory; these were the ones He delighted in. I could hear the softness

## A LITTLE PIECE OF HEAVEN

in His heart as He told of the working of His Holy Spirit at those times: trying to reach their hearts; softening the hardness, so that He could speak words that would make a difference. He spoke of His joy as the Holy Spirit broke through and His children turned to Him again, speaking out words of faith in their Father. Jesus told me how the angels rejoiced at these times and sang many songs of victory over the saints as they experienced their breakthrough. He spoke of the joy in the faces of His children, when the light of His life flooded their souls again.

# A New Place

As I looked at the face of Jesus, I could see that His countenance had changed. A wonderful brightness surrounded His face as He spoke these words:

"Blessed is the man who perseveres under trial, because when he has stood the test, he will receive the crown of life that God has promised to those who love him."

James 1:12

I realised that everyone I had seen on the mountain had persevered, but not all had passed through into the place of fullness in God. Those who settled for a basic belief in God without seeking His face, entered into the heavenly realms, but they forfeited what should have been theirs. The cost of truly following Jesus had become too great for many and for some, the pursuit of God had not even been considered; to settle for a place in heaven was all that they desired. I could see that they had received a crown of life, but they didn't receive the revelation of the fullness of God.

I could see *how easy it is to settle in a place that gives you satisfaction, even though much is forfeited by not being obedient to your call.* As I stood on this mountain, I could feel freshness come into my soul. I was in a new place in God: a place in which all of the things I thought I knew seemed like a shadow of the truth. My understanding of God was beginning to alter with each fresh encounter; my attitudes to my life as well as towards the lives of others were changing. It reminded me of the Scripture about the wine skins:-

> "And no-one pours new wine into old wineskins.
> If he does, the new wine will burst the skins, the wine will run out and the wineskins will be ruined.
> No, new wine must be poured into new wineskins.
> And no-one after drinking old wine wants the new,
> for he says, 'The old is better.'"
>
> Luke 5:37-39

So to receive deeper revelations of God, I must change my understanding of the ways of God and let go of the old way of thinking. This requires humility and openness to the renewing of my mind.

The Lord smiled at me and nodded approvingly as He acknowledged that I was beginning to understand this new place in Him. The mountain I was on represented the stages of growth in my Christian walk. I could see *the importance of maturing on earth for the fullness of God to inhabit us in our eternal home.*

With every level of heaven came a greater revelation of all that was waiting for us, as well as a greater knowledge of God. Those who allowed Him to change their "wineskin" (their fleshly attitude and desires) on earth were enabled to carry the full revelation and fullness of God in their eternal home. *God expresses His love for His children in equal measure, but the knowledge of Him differs for each person. Deeper knowledge of God means greater peace*

## A NEW PLACE

*and joy*. I was pleased to see that everyone was satisfied in this place and that there was no regret and no tears over what could have been.

Nevertheless, each one was aware that they could have had so much more if they had yielded to God on earth and fulfilled their purposes to the extent that God had planned. No one was allowed to enter a higher realm in heaven, so that they would remain content with their own reward. I stood in wonder at the plans of God for each one of us. I found it difficult to believe that I was blessed with the privilege of seeing what so many of my brothers and sisters in Christ had in store for them.

I understood the significance of the first level of heaven by the lake and yet I remembered desperately not wanting to leave. I wondered what else I was going to find in this place and I became excited at the prospect of all that was ahead. Jesus beckoned me forward and as we walked, the air became fresher. The glory of God increased upon me and a floating sensation took over as I became unaware of my body.

I could hear a new sound. It was the sound of drums loudly playing a sound of warfare and as I looked up I could see a group of drummers heading in our direction. The drumming was amazing; the beat of the drums began to deposit something deep into my heart. I could sense spiritual warfare for the saints on earth. I was drawn to walk alongside the drummers; as I joined them, I danced wildly. I had never danced like this before: I felt free as my arms went up and down to the rhythm of the beat. As the beat increased, I spun around and around, stomping my feet repeatedly; entering into warfare for the saints. The rhythm took over and I could feel my passion for the saints to win their battles increasing as I cried out for those who were struggling. I

## A LITTLE PIECE OF HEAVEN

shouted words of victory over each one of them.

The drums got louder and louder; I swirled in and out of the drummers, joined by other dancers. The emotions that were being expressed at this time were beyond words as the passion of the dancers increased. They weaved in and out of the drummers whilst punching the air as they cried out for the souls of those in trouble. After what seemed like an hour, the beat changed. A victory sound was heard and a cheer rippled through the dancers as they jumped up and down. I fell to my knees, humbly giving thanks for the times in my life that this same warfare had been fought over my life. All I could say was, "Praise You Lord; thank You."

If only I had received encouragement from the knowledge of this type of warfare taking place in the difficult times in my life.

Jesus stood at my side and stretched out His hand to lift me from my knees. The warmth of His hand expressed His friendship towards me which was always there and would never leave me. I walked with Him, as the rejoicing continued with shouts of victory echoing across the mountain for many more hours. Many of the saints who entered at this level had gone through many battles on earth gaining a deep knowledge of God and His ways. These were the saints that knew the strategies of the enemy and how to gain victory in God. The knowledge gained on earth was put to good use at this stage of the mountain.

I walked past many who had been intercessors on earth and who had fought spiritual battles for salvation and victory in many lives. So many of these intercessors waged war in the secret place; here they were being rewarded for their diligence and patience for their prayers for many. Much of the intercession was fought for those

## A NEW PLACE

who were weak from the battles or for the wayward and rebellious.

As I walked, I heard about many that came to this place and were shocked when they saw their reward. They had no idea that the work done in obedience to God throughout their lives resulted in such a reward. They simply acted out their faith. They often looked at those that appeared far more fruitful, consoling themselves with the thought that at least they would make it into heaven.

Jesus laughed as He told me about the days of shocked silence after they arrived in this place and the days of dancing that followed with joy filling their hearts. They diligently sought to please the Lord in all that their hands found to do; always believing that it wasn't enough. If they had sought the face of Jesus, they would have been released from this burden. They thought that this place in heaven was reserved for the mighty warriors of faith and the evangelists. The Lord told them that as long as His children were obedient to their calling, they would enter this place. The dancing went on for days with people from nations of the world. It was a joy to see the unity and the love between them.

Jesus spoke:

"So you see, My child, My burdens are easy and My yoke is light. Unfortunately, many of My children walk away from the simplicity of their call to follow other callings for which they are not gifted. They then walk away when the burden becomes too great or when they become dissatisfied.

"The enemy has deceived My flock and its leaders for a long time. I long for a people who will work out My purposes by My Spirit. When this happens, My children will be placed in the positions in which they are gifted. They will see fruit in the land; they will see My purposes fulfilled. They think that more fasting and more prayer will work. I watch and I wait for them to seek Me for My purposes while they waste many hours on fruitless tasks. I have given them the Bible to show them how to live; with stories of the saints of the Old Testament. Their mistakes are there for My children to see the consequence of sin and the importance of following Me. How much more can I do for My children?"

The Lord looked at me as we reached our destination. I could hardly contain my excitement as I saw the place of reward. I wanted to run but I would not leave Jesus.

A river appeared in front of me and it flowed with the beauty of life. A golden haze shimmered above its surface and the life of God was in it. I could see many precious stones of every colour; emerald, ruby, diamonds and pearls, sprinkled liberally at each side of the river. I wanted to sit and take it all in but the Lord encouraged me to walk beyond the river.

I walked and longingly looked at the precious stones; wanting to touch them as they sparkled in the sunshine. Jesus looked at me and said that He had so much more to show me. As we walked, the whole atmosphere around us changed, as I saw more and more saints surrounding us. They too marvelled at the stones and the river, but they were focused on what was ahead. I looked up and saw a throne embellished with precious stones. As we got closer, Jesus left my side and seated Himself upon the throne, with the angels surrounding Him. The angels clothed Him in a purple robe which was covered

## A NEW PLACE

in rubies, symbolising the blood of Calvary and His Kingship. I stepped away from the throne overwhelmed with feelings of unworthiness before Jesus as He sat on His throne in all of His majesty.

Jesus called me forward and uttered the words I needed to hear:

"I have called you friend, so draw close to Me regardless of My Kingship. The key to being a true King is to remain a servant and a friend."

I could see that *there should be no distinction between people of recognition and those without*. I had become accustomed to distancing myself from people of significance, as I had always found them interacting with those that they considered of equal significance.

*Jesus cut through these values and traditions of men, He was all embracing* and I now understood what it was to be a true follower of Christ. The longer I sat next to Him, the longer I felt a change happening on the inside of me. A feeling of empowerment came as a revelation of my identity in Christ flooded my soul. No earthly position could have made me feel the way I was feeling now. The realisation of all that I possessed in Christ sank deeper into my mind-set and I found it difficult to believe that I had fallen short of this knowledge on earth. To try and encourage my brothers and sisters in Christ to embrace this understanding would have been impossible. It had taken me a journey into the heavenly realms for me to understand and accept it. The feeling of being one with Jesus was overwhelming and the doubts about my identity disappeared. *It seems that our true feelings surface when we are faced with a challenge to our attitudes.*

As I thought about the times on earth when I had

acknowledged much of what was preached as truth, I realised that *theoretical knowledge alone is useless unless this truth is tested and becomes part of the foundations of your life. The words preached on a Sunday and elsewhere will not take root; unless you live them out and allow them to become part of who you are.* How I longed for the truths of God to become all that they should be in my life. To walk as a child of God and in His power meant I could pray for the sick and they would be healed and the emotionally scarred would be set free. These revelations and the changes that had taken place in my life so far had come at a cost, but the cost was nothing in comparison to a transformed life.

Jesus looked down at me and smiled as He acknowledged all of the things contained in my heart. He had a sceptre in His hand that had the authority to make significant changes on the earth. This authority was under the control of His Father until the time that had been ordained. There was tremendous power locked up inside the sceptre which was waiting to heal the nations. I longed to see it being used for its full purpose, even though I knew that the heart of God was locked up inside, brimming with compassion and love for those He longs to save. Jesus would only release its power when the hand of God allowed Him. I could see His palms sweating blood as He held it. He had the power to save the world from its present condition as He had done before. I watched God's heart beat through His Son Jesus, who had such passion for the lost and broken. I was silent as I beheld the Son with the sceptre and its power. Faith stirred in my heart.

I could see that the timing of this release of power was crucial. I stood there with complete faith in God the Father and the decisions He makes in all of our lives. *We strive to understand the delays in our earthly lives and why*

## A NEW PLACE

*prayers take so long to be answered. I stood here witnessing the hands of Jesus sweating blood as He waited to bring an end to the suffering in the world. I could see that His heart is breaking, for the promises of God to be fulfilled in our lives. His hand is restrained waiting for the right time. Not in our eyes, but in God's.*

After having the privilege of seeing this scene, it was time to move on and visit the places that Jesus had purposed. I bowed before the throne. I could not turn my back upon this sight as I would not see it again for some time. I wanted to keep this treasure locked up in my heart, so that I could share it with the nations of the world.

# Rubies, Diamonds and Hidden Treasures

I was tired, so I decided to rest before going any further. I returned to the river as I had not forgotten the colours of the precious stones on the banks. The grass looked green and healthy amidst an array of diamonds and rubies. Here was my resting place: beneath a willow tree. I looked at the river in front of me and watched it continually flowing with vibrant colours that mingled with one another. It was fascinating to watch as it created shades I had never seen before.

I looked at the stones on either side of the bank. On seeing that they had great significance, I asked that my spiritual eyes would be opened to their meaning.

These were the fruits of the Spirit that flowed from this river of life. Every so often, as the river flowed, one of these stones would be launched out of the water and onto the bank. I was amazed at their beauty but wisdom revealed that these stones were admired for more than their appearance. They were a heavenly representation of what took place on the earth, as the children of God flowed in the fruits of the Spirit.

## A LITTLE PIECE OF HEAVEN

"But the fruit of the Spirit is love, joy, peace, patience, kindness, goodness, faithfulness..."

Galatians 5:22

Heaven was creating a mirror image of the effect of the fruit displayed in the lives of God's people. I had not spent any time pondering the effect of a generous gesture or a kind word, as well as the many other expressions of love. *If we stopped and thought about the effect of one of these actions in the life of another person, we would try to operate in the fruits of the Spirit more often. Saying this, the fruits are not gifts we can simply manufacture. They stem from the life of God that flows through us. As the river flowed, it naturally birthed these precious stones. In the same way as we remain in the river of God we will naturally birth the fruits of the Spirit.* I lay down to take another look at this astounding sight and as the excitement of the day took its toll I fell asleep.

My guide gently shook me to wake me up. I was not startled as in previous encounters with those God would send my way. I had become accustomed to meeting my guide in so many different forms. The person smiled at me and as I rubbed my eyes and straightened my clothes I resisted the temptation to ask who my guide was, I just accepted that he was sent for a reason. My friend waited patiently for me to get ready and I became excited at yet another day with God. As I looked at the figure I saw that he was gentle and timid, which encouraged me to walk with him without instruction.

I walked at his side in silence. Every so often, he would look at me and smile meekly. I had never met anyone with such a quiet nature before: I wondered what my day with my new companion would hold. As I looked at him again, I saw a person that had completely yielded to the will of God. Someone that had been so changed by the workings of God in his life that he appeared to have no character left. His unassuming humble nature seemed to empty him of his character. I was confused as he didn't seem broken or scarred.

As I looked up, I could see that we were coming to a city in ruins, charred black by the fire that had consumed it. As I got closer, the buildings were smouldering and I could not understand why this place would be in heaven.

My guide told me that this place was a reminder to all who came here, of the devastation that is still upon the earth. Many here can get lost in experiencing heaven and forget that the earth is still groaning and yearning for victory. This place is visited by many to stir them to pray and see the world in its devastation; reminding them to intercede for the world until the end.

> The ruined city lies desolate;
> the entrance to every house is barred.
> In the streets they cry out for wine; all joy turns to
> gloom, all gaiety is banished from the earth.
> The city is left in ruins,
> its gate is battered to pieces.
>
> Isaiah 24: 10-13

On entering the ruins of this place I could smell the gut wrenching stench of rotting flesh. I wanted to run and hide but my guide told me that to truly see heaven, you have to see all of it. To capture the heart of God in this place, you must see the joy and the pain as well as the rewards and the judgements of God.

My guide told me that many on earth were in a place of naive Christianity. They told others about the benefits of the Kingdom, without telling them of the holiness that is expected and the righteous acts. He told me about the power God's children could have, if they walked in the fear of God instead of the fear of man. *The fear of God produces a natural desire to be holy and to perform righteous acts.* To expect the grace of God to cover continuous sin is foolish, and yet many are perishing because they are resting on God's grace instead of walking in the fear of Him. *God's grace covers His children, but it is not an excuse for sloppy Christianity. Grace has a time limit for those that take advantage of it, which results in them coming face to face with His discipline.*

As I looked at my guide, I saw strength in his face, which I had not previously noticed. I could see his passion rise from deep within for the people in the world.

"You think I look weak in comparison to other guides you have encountered."

I nodded in agreement.

"What the world sees as weakness is seen as strength in God's Kingdom. Holiness can sometimes appear weak in God's people; yet it produces calmness and peace in those that have it. There is no need to strive and show strength. I do not have to display my strength like a peacock; I can simply reveal it when it is needed. Outwardly strong people can cause those that are weak to shy away for fear of being crushed.

"One of the qualities that is lacking in God's people today is a quiet strength and the respect for those that have it. Those with a quiet strength are often overlooked, as their voices become lost in the noise and clamour. You must learn to listen for the quiet voice in a group: listen to what they say; as it often contains the wisdom of God. Those who refuse to fight to be heard are quite often the ones that have something to say that is worth listening to.

"When you read the New Testament you will see that Jesus rarely raised His voice to be heard in the market place, because it was the acts of healing that brought the crowds to listen to the One who had the power to change lives forever. You must nurture the quality of quiet strength in order to speak with wisdom, insight and understanding. It is more powerful than words."

As I looked deep into the eyes of my guide, I could see that he had terrific strength and a peace that I had not taken the time to notice. It made me realise that I must stop judging people by their outward appearance and to start discerning with my spirit. My guide smiled and told me about the pitfalls many of God's people had fallen into by taking notice of outward appearance;

"Those that look the least gifted may have hidden talents and simply need encouragement. Many of God's children have fallen by the wayside as their confidence has weakened. They see stronger characters being mentored or encouraged in the church and then disqualify themselves from a particular call.

"God's children have incredible gifts that are yet to be discovered and nurtured for the benefit of the Kingdom. In particular there are creative gifts which have been left dormant. But there is a new wave of the Spirit coming upon the church that will breathe the life of God onto these gifts and surprise many who have them. It will shock church leaders that have left these gifts undeveloped throughout church history.

"For leaders to truly walk with God, they must let go of their own limitations and resources and seek His face for the plans of God in the modern day church. God has the ability and the means to empower His people to reach the world in new, unique and creative ways with the message of the cross. The Gospel message has the power to save, if we seek God, He will enable us to reach the lost and draw them into our churches. It will not alter the Gospel message but it will be the bait to draw them in.

"Ministers and leaders must seek God's face more than ever before in the last days to stop the enemy building a dividing wall between His people and the world. The world is moving further away from God's truths. The church must not become distant and irrelevant to the young people of today. It must be courageous and be prepared to be a fool for Christ. Leaders must be prepared to risk all for the sake of the Gospel; submitting to the way in which they are called to lead and forsaking all else to run the race.

"There are few that run the race to the extent that He calls them, but the ones that do are His treasured possession. These are the ones that cause His eyes to be full of fiery passion as they fulfil His purpose on the earth. For those that run with their own ideas, God leaves them to it, but for those that follow Him, He gives the anointing and with it comes success and much fruit. The ones that look the most foolish can often be the ones that do His will, as they defy the intelligence of the intelligent by pursing Him with their whole heart and stepping out in faith. These are the ones who are persecuted, but they will receive the crown of life and a higher place in heaven. They are devoted to following and do not count the cost.

"They can go many years looking foolish in the sight of those they once walked with. And yet they have taken up their cross. God hears the lonely voice of these sheep who sometimes feel that they have lost their way. He reassures them in the watches of the night, that even though at present, they are not seeing the fruit of their walk; they will reap the blessings for obedience. They will see the fruit of their obedience, even if it takes many years. These are the ones who, when successful, receive a pat on the back by those that once frowned upon their actions."

My guide turned to me and told me that I needed time to take in all that he was showing me. As I sat amongst the dying embers of this city, I still hadn't completely understood why I was here; the full impact of this place had not yet entered my heart.

I was assured that I would not move on from this place, until I fully understood its relevance for my life and the lives of many on earth.

# Things are not what they seem!

I sat down and looked at the devastation. I could not ignore the stench that arose in my nostrils. I wanted to get away from this place, after experiencing so much of the goodness of God. Heaviness descended: I looked at my guide with feelings of desperation, but I knew I couldn't leave until I had understood the meaning of this place. As my countenance dropped, I started to weep.

My guide encouraged me to walk around the desolation while he explained all that I needed to know.

"People think that the darkness over the world is punishment for sin, but what they must realise is that even God's grace is found in darkness because without it, there would be no recognition of sin and its effect on lives. Unless the world sees the result of sin, they will not turn from their wickedness. So, what you can see in front of you is not as repulsive as you think.

"The stench that is an offence to your nostrils causes you to want to move away from this place. This is the effect that God wants to create in the world: the stench of sin. Many become sick of their sinful lives, but they struggle letting go when they are not shown a better way.

"This is why the church must start shining out as a

beacon for those that are searching. Unfortunately, many churches who are trying to be relevant and modern are not connecting the lost with their one true Saviour, Jesus Christ. It is only when the church seeks the face of God that they will know how to reach the world in a way that is modern and relevant but without compromise."

I looked again at this city that looked full of despair and sin and I saw it in a different light. I saw it as a city that had the potential to be saved: it mirrored the sin in the world. I had visited many beautiful cities in the world and stood in wonder at their architecture and different cultures. Yet wrapped up in it all was the side that I didn't see; sin and pain. *God sees it all and we turn away; acknowledging that we are powerless to help, except for prayer. I could see that unless people face the blackness of sin, nothing will ever change and people will not see a need for God. Governments continually pass laws that they hope will make a difference, but the world remains the same. Unless people see the destructive power of sin at work in the world, nothing would change.*

My guide prompted me to leave this place, now that its meaning had been revealed.

*When God gives revelation, He always moves us forward. God's children only remain in a place of stagnation because they are not learning anything new or they are resisting change. So, if you are ever frustrated at not moving on in your Christian walk, you must seek God for the reason.*

This city would remain in heaven until the Kingdom of God comes to earth.

I walked away with a deeper understanding of this place and my heart was uplifted as the darkness disappeared. The sound of music and the praises of people surrounded me; lightness started to come back into my heart. My guide became aware that I needed to get back to a place of peace and joy. He began to dance and as he danced he grabbed my hands and I could not help but join him. As we danced, I forgot all that had just taken place and the joy of the Lord bubbled up from within. *Oh, what peace we forfeit for not remaining in His presence!*

I entered a new part of the walk: flowers appeared amongst the grass and the sky became a deeper blue. The further we moved from the city, the more beautiful the land appeared and as the birds flocked overhead, the life of Christ abounded in all that we saw.

We walked for a few hours, until we came to a brook where we sat down to rest. The brook was crystal clear and the rocks beneath were covered in mildew and moss. I wondered how the water could remain clear as it surged over the top. Even the grass that grew amongst the rocks remained healthy and green. I watched the water flow down the brook. There were times when it would pass through a very narrow gap between two big rocks. As the water hit the rocks it piled up, splashing and covering the rocks either side with a spray. As it passed through the other side, the water became calm. Wisdom revealed to me that *it was a picture of our life in God. When we feel hemmed in by the pressures of life, it can seem that whether we turn to the left or right we cannot move forward. But just as the water in the brook always finds a way through the hard places, so will we, and we will eventually come to a place of rest. The answer is to find the path of least resistance (to God) and for some, this can mean repeatedly going in the wrong direction until we find the narrow path to freedom. We must know the seasons we are in and learn when to rest and seek God.*

The warmth of the sun and the peace of the brook caused me to fall asleep. I awoke a while later to find that

## A LITTLE PIECE OF HEAVEN

my guide had gone, so I decided to walk alongside the brook and watch the water wind its way down the bank. I had taken many walks like this and enjoyed talking to God, pouring out all that I had in my heart. I walked for a long time along the grassy banks and found such peace and satisfaction from knowing that I would spend eternity in this place.

# The Call and the Cost

As the brook disappeared in the ground beneath, I looked up and saw a vision of Jesus on the cross surrounded by a glow of glory. I began to worship. The glow became brighter and brighter, until rays of light poured forth. These rays revealed the power that was released at the time Jesus died. With every ray of light, there was a different victory to be found as they each represented the power of the cross for Salvation. There were so many shafts of light I could not count them all.

The revelation of the power of the cross was found in each ray of light, and I could see a yearning in the heart of Jesus for His brothers and sisters on earth to truly know this power. The heart of Jesus cried out for the sons and daughters to rise up and take their place on the earth. The power that came from Jesus was tangible.

I reached out to touch a beam of light that I knew contained the anointing for healing; it felt like electricity was passing through my body. I stood to my feet and tentatively moved closer, until wisdom told me to be bold and take what had already been paid for on the cross. I stepped forward again and placed my hand in a ray of light, which contained breakthrough for spiritual bondages. I felt another surge of power passing through me, which caused me to shake as it was released. Again and again, I placed my hands in the rays of light and the power of God flowed through me with such intensity.

I fell to the ground and God spoke:

"Take this power back with you. It is not for you or your glory; you are a vessel that I am sending to the nations to release My power and set My people free. This power is available to all of those that yield their lives to Me."

As the vision disappeared, I remembered how, over many years, I had longed to pray for people with the power of God flowing through me for the breaking of strongholds. For the first time since I had been here, I suddenly had the desire to return and minister to the hurting and the sick. I was glad because I was beginning to think of others more than myself. I became excited at the prospect of returning to earth and ministering to people; seeing them released from their bondages. My heavenly encounters were changing me and I was pleased that I would return a better person. Thoughts of returning quickly passed as the joy of being here took over, I didn't feel it was time to leave just yet.

I sat up startled, seeing that I was surrounded by many other people that had been brought to this place for the same reason. My heart had changed from the beginning of my journey; I was now relieved to know I was not alone and that I could share it with others. All of us had encountered God in different ways, but we were all here for the same reason: to receive empowerment for our purpose in the world. My heart rejoiced as I realised that this was a unique moment in the life of the church. God was calling His people to encounter Him in ways that were rare. It encouraged me to know that many

## THE CALL AND THE COST

were being called to this place as God prepared ministers of the Gospel, who could operate at a higher level of anointing. God showed me that all those He brought here had longed for this encounter over many years; this was their fulfilment. Even though we had all seen different parts of heaven, at different times, God brought us all together in His perfect timing. He wanted us to witness one another receive the power, which He had longed to release upon those that had laid down their lives. God allowed each of us to go on a journey in which we died to our ambitions and desires; realising that our destiny was greater. This was birthed in us through the workings of God over a long period of time. When each of us faced our natural longings and desires, we were able to say, "I know I have a higher calling."

Each of us knew that as God saw the birthing of Christ within us, He was going to take us on to greater things.

As we gathered together, we exchanged our stories to share what we had learnt. It felt as though it was a big party and we celebrated the privilege of being here. Each story was wonderful; a pattern was emerging within each one of us as we shared the battle to submit our ways to God. We all agreed that one of the biggest stumbling blocks was a lack of understanding and that the less we understood, the more we resisted God and hardened our heart to His ways. We all realised that if we had yielded sooner and trusted God, even when we didn't understand, we would have had more peace and less battling.

The maturity of these saints was wonderful to see: I had not encountered many Christians who had grown to this level. I looked at their faces and I could see the beauty of the Lord in them, in the same way my guide had shown me the beauty within me, earlier in my journey. It was easier to appreciate the beauty of the Lord in the faces of others. To truly be able to love, I had to love myself and the beauty that God had created within. I could see the workings of Christ manifested in the young and old. God had renewed the youth of the older saints, physically as well as spiritually. As we exchanged stories about our lives on earth, we could see that each of us acted out our faith in completely different ways. Some were in the workplace, feeling a particular calling in their field of work and others were in a simple job that didn't require a particular ability or skill, but were called to be a witness in that place to the many they would meet. Others were ladies who were called out of the workplace; to be full-time mothers and to reach out to other parents as well as being devoted to prayer.

There was such an astounding mix of callings. It was fascinating to see the wisdom of God weaving His intricate plans for His people. I could see how His complex tapestry had weaved its way through lives as I heard stories of these saints and the battles each one had encountered. Many of these battles included doubt and financial pressures, which had come to each one to force them away from their calling at that stage of their life. The consequent victories revealed the hand of God, at every stage of their journey, bringing them to a place of peace. I felt the tension as they shared their last minute answers to prayer for finances, much to the delight of those listening. They felt as though they were stepping off a cliff when the pressure was at its worst and yet to turn to other means of provision meant defeat. With each testimony there were similar stories of faith. I loved hearing each person share their similar experience. They actually felt a spiritual path appear as they were faced

## THE CALL AND THE COST

with making a leap into a place of complete trust in God, in the midst of impossible circumstances. Each one faced the possibility of perishing in their struggle for the sake of their calling, but as they let go of their fear and trusted God, the breakthroughs came. I shared my identical story and even though it was a frightening experience, we all agreed that it was also exhilarating. We had all come to the end of ourselves and had stepped into a new place in God. I remembered the story of Ruth when she was asked to speak to the king on behalf of the Jewish nation. As she faced death for the sake of her people she said,

"And if I perish, I perish."

Esther 4:16

Ruth didn't perish. God answered her prayer and the Jewish nation was saved. As I remembered this powerful piece of Scripture, the names of many more Bible characters that had acted in the same way flashed before me.

David could have killed his enemy Saul in the cave as he cut off the corner of Saul's robe:

"He said to his men, 'The LORD forbid that I should do such a thing to my master, the LORD's anointed, or lift my hand against him; for he is the anointed of the LORD.'"

1 Samuel 24:6

David left the fate of Saul to God, because to take matters into his own hands would have showed his lack of trust in God's sovereign hand upon his life as well as Saul's.

Peter wanted to save Jesus from the cross:

"Peter took him aside and began
to rebuke him 'Never, Lord!' he said.

## A LITTLE PIECE OF HEAVEN

'This shall never happen to you!'

Jesus turned and said to Peter, 'Get behind me, Satan!
You are a stumbling block to me;
you do not have in mind the things of God,
but the things of men.'"

Matthew 16:22-23

Daniel faced death as he was thrown to the lions and his friends faced death in the fiery furnace. Each one of them refused to bow to the idol Nebuchadnezzar had made. Facing death rather than dishonouring God and they were rescued in the midst of their suffering.

In each of these stories, each person could have saved themselves. But because they had the purposes of God at the forefront of their mind, to take matters into their own hands would have caused their level of faith to stagnate.

*God tests our faith in Him and when we fail a test we cannot move on. We will continue to come across the same test over and over again until we pass through in victory.* The people around me discussed how important it was for all of God's children to pass the tests to enable us to move into our calling. As we talked, we could see how Abraham had to pass this test, before he entered the land of Canaan. He prepared to sacrifice his son, Isaac. He didn't try to understand why; he simply trusted that God's ways were higher. We could all see that *this pureness of heart - to the ways and purposes of God - must become part of who we are, to enable us to become all that God requires. There must be no shadow of turning in us, just as there is no shadow of turning in God.*

"Every good gift and every perfect gift is from above, and cometh down from the Father of lights, with whom

## THE CALL AND THE COST

is no variableness, neither shadow of turning."

James 1:17 KJB

I looked at my friends and realised that we had all passed through this place into a place of victory. We jumped to our feet praising God for His ways and His victory in our lives. We remained in this place of praise for many hours and were joined by many who had gone before us on this journey of faith and who now called heaven their home.

# A Canopy Under the Stars

I looked around to see the scene changing as the Spirit of God surrounded us. We could see His presence rising from the ground beneath. Every tangible thing that we saw rejoiced. Even the rocks were shaking and the light shone brighter. The praises of God were heard across heaven, filling the atmosphere. We all gathered and said our farewells. We wondered if we would remember one another as we returned to earth. We knew that one day we would be here again, rejoicing in all that God had achieved through our lives. We waved goodbye until we were out of sight.

As the sun set, a golden glow on the horizon refused to let the night take its place. The beauty of the day became locked in my memory as I remembered the stories of the saints. My heart was glad. I was part of a new generation of saints that were being taken up into heavenly places, to take back that which would benefit the saints in the last days.

The last of the glowing horizon disappeared. I could see a small canopy in front of me, held up by sticks. I got closer; I could see that it was old and torn; it could barely stay up. It was so bedraggled that it was hardly worth sitting underneath its fragile and grubby frame. Nothing in me wanted to sleep under here, but I felt compelled to sit a while in its shelter. I sat down and remained upright and cross legged for some time, until I realised I was here for the night, so I thought I might as well relax. I sat looking out onto a sky of stars, which glistened so brightly. Some were clustered together in large areas whilst others shone out on their own. It was mesmerizing and as I looked at them I could see that the beauty of those that were on their own were not as stunning as the clusters. The single stars looked out of place, as if they should be part of the clusters. It reminded me of a season in my life in which God had taken me out of the church and into what appeared to be a lonely place.

Then God's voice broke through the silence,

"Those that follow Me must learn to exist for a period of time without the covering and support of the Church to enable them to understand My ability to be their strength and supply in all circumstances. For those that have taken this step, many feel as though they have been abandoned. They become insecure and in the same way you have just looked up at the covering above your head and seen its inadequacy, My children feel the same way without the Church.

"In this season, I unearth all of these insecurities. To continue in a position of strength on this journey of faith, they must remove the things that have been holding them up. They have created a deceptive covering that can never replace the covering I can give you. If the people of God can only function when surrounded by the church, there is something lacking. To allow Me to reveal Myself as your only source will result in a life transformed. Those that learn to completely rely on Me will be strengthened. They will be able to speak with more confidence about

## A CANOPY UNDER THE STARS

Me and what I have become in their lives.

"Many of My ministers think that not being part of a church for any length of time is not right. Yet these times are used for growth. Clusters of stars stand out far more than a single star, but can also get lost in their collective brightness; instead of shining out as an individual. Many of My children cling to the church in the hope that they will gain recognition in their gifting from church leaders. This can cause them to be stunted in their growth, instead of relying on Me for guidance and the next step. Many have waited far too long for the chance to prove themselves in their gifting. The only recognition My children need is from Me. Their confidence should come from Me. They must stop looking for recognition from people. I will bring them to a place in which they can function in their gifting."

I remembered my younger days in church life and I thought of the times when I longed to do more and to be used by God to a much greater degree. I had lots of ideas but looking back, I didn't have the strength or the maturity to hold all that God had placed in my heart. And so God took me out of church life for a season to nurture, teach and bring out all of the qualities, for the purposes He had ordained for me. I understood why I had been encouraged to sit under this canopy and as I looked at it again, I could see that it represented the humility of Christ and our willingness to sit at the feet of the Master and receive all that He had to give.

At that time, I found it hard to believe that I could exist outside of the church and how He alone could be enough. This season caused my roots to go much deeper into God and I learnt to solely rely on Him for all of my needs. The protection and covering (that I had previously thought best for me), provided me with little ability to cope with all that I would encounter in life. To completely trust in God's ability to provide all that I needed, emotionally, spiritually and even practically, proved to be a much better choice. In fact, it was the only one.

As I looked up, the canopy above my head had changed into a golden cloth, shimmering in the moonlight. It was no longer held up by sticks but by solid gold rods.

I sat in awe at the wisdom and ways of God and I wondered how I could ever doubt the ways in which He changed me.

The sky looked black but beautiful. It highlighted how God had called each one of us, to shine out like stars in the dark world in which we lived. I rested my head underneath, what was now, a golden canopy and I felt surrounded by the love of God as I fell into a deep sleep. As I slept, I felt secure in the knowledge that God surrounded me and that I was at a significant point in my journey with Him. This revelation enabled me to see that *this is what He wants for all of His children. God wants us to get to a place where we completely trust Him for every aspect of our lives, which consequently transforms us into people whose confidence, is in Him alone.*

# God's Chosen Vessels

I slept soundly as the storm clouds gathered over my head.

I awoke to the sound of the wind swirling around the canopy; the skies appeared heavy with rain, so I jumped up to run for shelter. My surroundings changed so rapidly that feelings of security faded and I knew I must guard my peace. I had encountered many extreme changes in life and one of my biggest weaknesses was to react to these changes and to lose my peace.

As I ran ahead looking for cover, I came across an old man at the roadside. He really was in a sorry state. All I wanted to do was pass him by. There was nothing in his appearance that was welcoming and nothing about him encouraged me to speak to him. As I tried to pass by on the other side still looking for shelter, I remembered what I was taught about not using my discernment and responding to appearances. And so, in the middle of the storm with the rain clouds about to burst, I stopped and looked at the old man and used the spirit of discernment to reveal his true nature. As I looked, his appearance became of no consequence. The beauty I saw within made me draw closer to hear what he had to say:

"Aha, at last you have learnt to discern before judging

## A LITTLE PIECE OF HEAVEN

and to be open to the Holy Spirit's guidance. Many of God's children can bypass those they are meant to meet because they are so consumed with their own lives. This is a test of the heart for all of God's children: to remain in peace regardless of circumstances and to listen to the Holy Spirit."

As I looked at the figure again, I could see that his appearance was changing and the longer I looked, the more he changed. The more I used my discernment the more I could see his beauty being brought to the surface. This was God showing me what He wanted me to see, not just in this man, but in all of His people. This gift of discernment would empower me to see people in a different light and to celebrate their giftings and the beauty of who God had called them to be. I would also be able to encourage them and build their confidence as I brought affirmation of the qualities that I saw.

The figure smiled and spoke approvingly,

"Well done! You have finally learnt that, even when focused on yourself, you can give your time to other people. From now on, you will be more open to those God sends your way and you will be open to the Holy Spirit's direction. The key is to never be so focused on what you are trying to achieve that you either bypass or ignore those people God sends your way. Now walk with me, my child, and I will show you some more."

I felt such warmth and peace coming from this old man and as I walked, I remembered the times in my life when God had sent older people into my life, simply to be a blessing. I had gained so much from time spent with this wonderful generation of God's people. With many of them displaying such warmth and love that has surrounded me all of my life.

As I walked, I listened to the stories that this man had to tell me. He told me about the Old Testament characters and the stories they shared about their lives in God. He spoke of their exploits which are not recorded in the Bible and their shock at entering heaven to find that their failures are not recorded. He shared of their joy at meeting Jesus, the promised Messiah and the rejoicing of the saints as they enjoyed the full revelation of the Scriptures that Isaiah spoke of concerning Jesus. It was wonderful to hear about their days of rejoicing as they embraced the full revelation of their lives. How wonderful it must have been as they heard about the impact their acts of faith had on their own generation, as well as future generations.

I was told about their reaction as they realised that they were part of the family line of David and consequently Jesus, they fell on their knees in awe and wonder. The saints rejoiced as they understood the meaning of the Cross for those that believed. Their eyes were opened to the fullness of its power to save and change lives. I was told about the tears that were shed as they understood that we were all brothers and sisters in Christ and that they were part of a long heritage of saints that would inherit eternal life.

The old man lit a fire and insisted that I joined him to listen to more stories about the struggles of faith and the times when the saints doubted God. He spoke of the angels and the intercession that would go hand in hand at these times of doubt. He spoke of the frustration of the Father, when He knew that all that was required of His children was to believe in the purpose and promises of God for their lives. He shared the times of defeat and the deception of the enemy to win the souls of men; he also told of the continuous rejoicing of the angelic hosts as they celebrated the victories of many. The old man prepared a meal for both of us and as the fire roared he cooked all that he had brought. I listened in wonder at the battles of the Old and New Testament characters. I lost track of time and I quickly forgot the shelter that I had been seeking from the storm, which had now passed. Wisdom spoke into my heart and revealed that this was an example of many times *I had tried to deal with battles on my own instead of being led to a place of peace by God; leaving Him to deal with the problems. All I had to do was to continue being obedient to all that had been asked of me. The blessing is in the obedience, and when we get this right, the problems that surround us fall away.* The meal was so satisfying and the company was delightful, I couldn't imagine anywhere else I would rather be.

I melted into this comfort as I continued to listen to all he had to share. My mind was being renewed as I sat at his feet. I didn't have to ask any questions because just when I was about to ask, the man replied with the answer. This was a special time; one that I would never forget and from now on my times with God would be more like this: simply sitting and listening. As time passed by, we both decided that it was time to move on and we bid each other goodbye.

As I left his side, I walked through a field and God's creation came alive. I delighted in the birdsong: the scenery was bright and colourful. Everything was full of life. The flowers covered the ground like a carpet and I could not help but walk over them. I was surprised to find that they bounced back up, unharmed and perfect. My garden on earth was full of plants that quite often struggled to survive with roses that were continually covered in black flies. I found it difficult to believe that I was standing amongst nature that didn't spoil or die and that this was how it was supposed to be. I could see from this that the more you surround yourself with what is normal for you; the less likely you are to believe anything different. I looked at nature around me and thought how wonderful it would be if this was reality. Wisdom spoke within and told me that this was real and my own knowledge of nature wasn't. Sadness entered my heart, as this scene not only mirrored all that should have been in nature, but also in our lives. I could see how far we were from the truth of what our lives should have been and how much we have missed out on, because of sin.

God's voice spoke within me:

"Even though you feel that you have missed out on earth because of sin, I work together in all things to those who love God and are called to His purposes. I work in nature to cause you to see the beauty in all things - even in death. With every death there is new life. Even in the dying there is beauty because what is not needed any longer is being taken away and it is being replaced by something that is. So you see My child; I am in control of all things."

Sadness left me; my heart was gladdened at having wisdom as my constant guide to bring me back in line with the ways of God. The more I thought about the ways which God had spoken to me, the closer I felt to God. *Wisdom is not separate from God; it is part of who He is.* I felt privileged to have the wisdom of God living on the inside of me, as well as the blessing of encountering wisdom in its many different guises along my journey. I could see that the form in which wisdom appeared was important to me. God often sent a certain type of person to me, with a message I needed to hear at just at the

# A LITTLE PIECE OF HEAVEN

right time. The wrong person with the right advice could spoil the message, just the same as the right person with the wrong advice can spoil it. How often have I passed by those sent to help me because their mannerisms offended me or I simply didn't relate to them?

I remembered a time when I became disinterested in the teaching of a guest speaker in my church. After the message was over, my friends were saying how great it was. I prayed and asked God why I didn't receive anything from it.

God spoke to me and said,

"You didn't receive from him because you thought he was a boring preacher and your spirit closed down. I can deliver a message that you need to hear through any person in anyway and at anytime in your life. Do not be offended by the vessel that I use."

# A Sea of Faces

As I moved through the flowers, their fragrance overwhelmed me. I was consumed with the smell and could hardly think straight due to their pungent aroma. It was beautiful, but it became so overpowering that all I could do was lie down in the middle of them. The flowers felt soft, as if I was lying on cotton wool. I stared up at the sky and felt that I could stay here for hours, as all of my thoughts drifted away. The pungent smell changed into a sweet smelling fragrance. Thankfully, I had learnt the difference between entering God's rest and my normal way of resting. To rest in the Holy Spirit brought refreshment to my soul. *Resting in God was intended to be a joy for all of His children.* My head felt as though it was sinking into the petals that surrounded me and as I looked up I saw a sea of faces coming towards me. Amongst them were the faces of people I had lost many years earlier; they were all smiling. Those who didn't know me, continued past to meet with the saints they knew.

My dad suddenly appeared in front of me, I could see that his face was bright and different to what I remembered. I was overwhelmed by seeing him and my welcome must have been somewhat subdued, as I simply reached out with limp arms. I rested my head on his

## A LITTLE PIECE OF HEAVEN

shoulder and breathed a sigh of relief, as I saw him in this place. I hid my head in his shoulder, as I didn't want him to see my tears.

It was a surreal moment and even though we know we will see our loved ones in Christ again, it was a privilege to be able to see them now. As I turned in the other direction, there was my husband standing with arms wide open, with a welcoming joy all over his face. I was speechless. I had never seen such an expression on his face and as my husband took me in his embrace, I felt a peace that cannot be explained in words as I acknowledged that he was where he was supposed to be. I was shocked by my feelings towards them as they no longer played the roles of father or husband; they were simply two people that I loved very much. Our roles towards one another had ended and all that remained was a simple bond of love.

Other relatives greeted me including my grandparents, a great aunt, an auntie and an uncle and I had the same reaction towards all of them. The love we had for one another was incredible and it was a love I had not known on earth, with heartfelt friendship towards one another. This was not what I expected. We all spent many hours talking about our heavenly experiences and the joy of being in this place. Their joy knew no bounds and they explained that they were not all in the same place in heaven, but that God had called them to be with me for this allotted time before they returned.

I desperately wanted to know if we all spent eternity together, or if these different places in heaven meant separation. They each assured me that we were together, but had different roles to play and for some of the time we were apart. I didn't completely understand what they were telling me, but they were all so full of joy and contentment, that I did not feel the need to question them any longer.

This was the second stage of my journey in heaven and God wanted to bless me with meeting those that I had lost many years before. They assured me that it would not be long before we would all be together again and that time was of no relevance to them now. I found this whole concept - of time being irrelevant - very difficult to understand. For me, time was very important, as it was to all of mankind. I had come from a world in which people crammed so much into one day that it caused each day to become a blur of activity.

As the tears rolled down my cheeks, family members gathered around to assure me that there was no need to feel sad. I had stepped into eternity the moment I became a Christian, but for now I had to live in a different place to them. They encouraged me with thoughts of our wonderful reunion and with the understanding that on entering heaven, we would all be one big family. As we waved goodbye, I felt my tears beginning to dry up and my greater understanding of eternity took away the pain of separation.

As my relations disappeared, I felt as though my thoughts on life were being turned upside down. The presence of God made those moments that would normally have been heart wrenching into pleasant ones. I realised that it *is all about our perspective on our lives and our future. The more we think that our earthly life matters more than anything else, the more devastating it is when we make mistakes and fail.* In this place, those moments of failure in life were so insignificant in the face of all that I had seen here.

I thought about how wonderful it would be if I could pass on all that I had learnt here. These lessons would enable people to move on much faster from failures and heartache, as well as so many other road-blocks that cause people to come to a standstill. I could see that every obstacle would be removed if people knew what I know now. *Every difficulty would be seen in the light of eternity and every trial would be seen for what it is: a tool for God to develop us into the people He knows we can become.*

I was grateful to God for this journey to heaven and to know that all of those I had lost were full of joy and contentment. But the more I thought about it, I began to feel dismay that the saints in heaven were not more concerned with the pain and suffering in the world. Those people in the world that had lost loved ones spent much time grieving: yet those that were here had no pain, no suffering and definitely no grief. Dismay turned to exasperation as it appeared that the loss of their earthly life meant little after entering the heavenly realms. In contrast those left behind had all of the difficulties of life to contend with.

So many people grieve over what loved ones will not experience, but all I had seen here showed me that once entering heaven, little thought was given to their past life. They simply rejoiced in the fact that they would see loved ones again. For the most part we grieve our own loss of loved ones but many experience grief for the years lost by those that have died at a young age.

I was not happy at all and I left this place feeling very disgruntled. As I walked away, my heart grew hard, as I thought of how happy my relatives had been and how completely unconcerned they were with the affairs of the world.

Just at that moment, I felt an arm surround my shoulder and a great love swamped my soul, which melted the hardness. I turned around to see a friend of mine smile at me and as he spoke, my emotions got the better of me and I cried. This great friend was the old man I had met earlier, who was sent to give me understanding.

"You see, even though it appears as if we are all complacent and unconcerned with what happens in the lives of people on earth, you couldn't be further from the truth. We spend much of our time in prayer; interceding for those who will inherit eternal life and those who are experiencing great battles. Because we didn't speak about it, it doesn't mean that we are unconcerned. We find that to focus on how wonderful heaven is and soak ourselves with joy, results in us having a greater enthusiasm to pray for those that are lost. So please don't leave with the wrong impression of our lives here. We love those on earth and simply look forward to the day when there are new heavens and a new earth and we will all be together."

At this, the old man left my side.

I felt guilty as I walked away, but I quickly got rid of this feeling, as this was not the purpose of his conversation with me. I walked for many miles. I thought how wonderful it will be when Jesus returns and the final trumpet blows, to signal the last of the world as we know it. And I thought about the new heavens and the new earth and I became excited at the prospect of everything being made new with no more tears and no more crying. I looked at the place where I was standing and wondered if what I was seeing was an exact representation of the new world. It was impossible to fathom all that it would be, but I knew that the people who inhabited it would no longer be fighting with sin in their lives. The purity of mankind would be something to behold not only in men,

# A LITTLE PIECE OF HEAVEN

women and children, but also in creation itself.

I walked for a long time, remembering the faces of those I had seen here; marvelling as I thought about how fresh and renewed their features looked as they spoke of their joy. I remembered many of their lives on earth and some of the difficulties they had encountered. I became filled with delight for each one that spoke of their joy as they found themselves in paradise.

# The Throne Room

The scenery around me quickly changed. I felt as though I was being taken up this mountain to another new place in heaven. The lightness that entered my spirit was unlike any other and as I was taken up higher, I felt as though I was no longer in my body. I was in the Spirit and even though I felt that this should be an unnerving experience it wasn't. I remembered the times I had heard about people having out-of-body experiences, but nothing would have ever prepared me for this. The higher I went, the brighter the scenery. In fact, everything became so full of light that all I could see was brightness. As I looked ahead, I saw a throne. Upon it was the vague appearance of a man sitting with a sceptre in His hand. I was instructed to move towards the throne. I moved forward and I came to rest at the feet of God. God was Spirit; yet He knew that I needed to see Him in human form.

No words were needed as we exchanged thoughts about my time in heaven. I was beginning to embrace all that I was learning on this journey and I knew that many changes were taking place in me, which would enable me to be more effective on my return to earth.

I sat for many hours, at the feet of the One who knew me and formed me in my mother's womb. The One that knew my future, my past and the reasons I had been brought to this place. I could barely bring myself to speak. So I spent this time soaking in His presence and enjoying being at the feet of the Creator of heaven and earth.

As I looked at His face with its kindly countenance and knowing smile, I felt such peace and yet I could not fully comprehend the nature of God and knew that I never would. He spoke about all that He would accomplish in and through the lives of His people. He told me of His pride in His children who lived lives in complete humility and obedience to all that He had required of them; He spoke of the rewards that were theirs. I was surrounded by the wonders of heaven and the realities of the different levels. I did not even consider that I would be shown the hidden places of heaven, as I did not feel worthy of this great honour.

Knowing my thoughts God spoke to me in an audible voice;

"My child, do you really think that you have seen the treasures in this place because you were worthy. You have seen it because I have chosen you, it is because of My call on your life; it is your destiny. If you do not understand this, you will not understand the nature of the cross. I did not send Jesus because you were worthy. I sent Him because I love the whole human race. How can a Father not love what He has created? Just as you love your own children, I love Mine, but so much more. My heart aches for the world to understand My love - expressed through My Son, Jesus, and through all those who are His. So it is not about worthiness; it is about love. I have been revealing My love to you in this place of heaven, so that you can go back and share all that you have seen and the treasures that await My loved ones."

## THE THRONE ROOM

I fell back, as His love consumed me like a wave in the ocean. This tremendous love of God caused me to forget the questions I thought I would ask about the world and its pain. I could see that perfect love really did cast out all fear and I realised that my questions showed a lack of trust in God and who He was. The trust that came into my heart replaced all the unanswered questions. I accepted that the answer to each question was "GOD IS LOVE".

I started to laugh as I imagined the many mouths that would be closed as they encountered the love of God: the many questions that would never be asked. I loved the completeness I felt while sitting at the feet of God.

He then told me that it was time to visit the special places in heaven and that I would have a guide. I suddenly felt a presence behind me: it was time to go. I bowed and waved goodbye as my guide directed me forward. As I came to a standstill, my guide encouraged me to pass through the door and to enter this new place.

As I did so, I felt a cold wind blowing all around me. It felt icy; but refreshing as the saints in glory surrounded me. I don't know how, but I recognised each one of them; they beckoned me forward. Each saint began to tell me about the treasures in this place and the rewards that were given to those who came here. They told of the joys and peace, as well as the abounding love. The saint's rewards came in unique packages to suit each individual character. So for those that were blessed with artistic talents, they were given the privilege of creating the most wonderful masterpieces of art as their gifts and abilities exceeded their wildest dreams. These gifts were not limited to art work and sculptures: they were taken to places in which they were allowed to make designs for new species of animals and plant life, all of which were taken to God to be perfected and approved by Him. I was amazed that in the new heavens God worked *with* people to create new species. I thought creation was reserved for God!

Those that had gifts of communication were allowed to create new ways of expressing love. For those that had the gift of encouragement; they simply enjoyed being alongside those with creative gifts and brought encouragement and help when it was needed. I saw how great God's plans were for the human race.

I was taken into many rooms, and in each one there was a new revelation of God and what He had planned for His children. I could not take in all the details of this higher place in heaven, as it had been meticulously planned by God to bless His children. I could not contain all that I was seeing; I simply hoped that I would remember most of it on my return. Even so, I was astounded that I was being shown so much and as I looked in each room I was reminded that I had only seen a fraction of what was possible in the next life.

There was one room that contained precious stones in which there were colours that were constantly changing. These stones looked as though they were living organisms. The colours constantly changed as they flowed around the stone. I could see that they represented an array of emotions that God had intended for the human race to feel. But because of sin, these emotions were locked up in these spiritual stones, waiting to be released into the lives of those that came here. My mind was limited to the emotions I had already experienced and I did not have the capacity to imagine any new ones. As I thought this, my guide encouraged me to place my hand on one of the stones. As I did, my mind exploded with so many emotions, that I quickly withdrew my hand and

## THE THRONE ROOM

moved away. I did not recognise any of the feelings and I was shocked to even consider that I would feel one new emotion, let alone all that was contained in one stone.

My guide called me forward to the next door of heaven. This door looked ancient and it symbolised a passage of time which had limited use. I stared at the door and tried to discern its meaning. But the longer I stared, the less I could discern, until my guide encouraged me to go through and find out more. As I walked through, I felt as though I had gone back in time instead of into heaven. I passed through this place expecting to meet people that could explain its meaning and as I looked ahead, I saw saints that were gathered together having an intense conversation. They all had their backs to me and so I pushed through the crowd to listen more closely. The saints were discussing someone that had just entered into the heavenly realms and were deciding the place in heaven in which this new saint should reside.

I was horrified to think that the fate of the saints was in the hands of anyone other than God. I thought that only God was able to decide this most important answer in the life of each person. As my thoughts were perceived by those around me, the crowd turned around and looked at me with eyes of fire and passion for God's people and I realised that I had upset these saints.

One who had authority began to shed some light on this scene.

"Do not think that we are deciding if the saints are good enough to join the highest ranks of heaven. We are discussing why each person wouldn't be allowed in the highest place. Our heart is that all join us in this place and we do not want any less for each of God's children than we ourselves have inherited. We do not care if those that inherit eternal life deserve to be here; we simply want all to be here.

"Nothing that we say or do will make any difference to where they will end up going, but we are those that God is going to use to rule and reign in the new heavens and the new earth. So while we are here, we make use of the time we have by learning as much as we can about God and His ways. We all must experience the judgement seat of Christ and after facing our own errors and wrongdoing, we want to do our best to rule and reign in the new heavens and earth. So we will be learning His ways until the return of the King."

I felt as though I had offended them by my thoughts and I apologised as I walked away. One of them called me back and told me that they did not get offended; they simply wanted me to see that they were passionate about their calling. I stood next to a lady who encouraged me forward saying, "Would you like to join us?" I was not sure if I wanted to be involved in all that was taking place, but I told them I was willing to watch and learn. There were a number of ladies in the group as well as men and they all had great respect for one another. I was pleased to see men and women leading with equal importance as I had not encountered this level of willingness to work together on the earth. I could see that each of them understood the different qualities and roles they played in the lives of people. They each stood back and let the other one pass their opinion at exactly the right time and on the specific subject that they would be more qualified to judge. It was like watching a classical orchestra play the most wonderful tune called, "The Wisdom Of God". I stood in amazement as they came to

## THE THRONE ROOM

their conclusions about each of the lives that had been presented to them in this place.

Many of these saints had withstood the trials and tribulations of life and had held on until the very end through some of the greatest difficulties.

There could be no greater honour and responsibility for the saints in glory than to see the wisdom of God in action, in the lives of those over whom they were commissioned to rule and reign. These saints were learning deep truths of God. I found it difficult to stand amongst them. Their calling was great and I shuddered as I stood in awe of the roles to which they had been assigned. I thought about all of the people that I knew in Christ and wondered who would be seated in this place in heaven, even though it was impossible to fathom.

As I stood back from this intense discussion, an arm drew me in to encourage me to listen a while longer. The lady drew my attention to a particular discussion and asked me to be aware of the heart of those talking, rather than the content of the discussion. So I listened.

I then had the most wonderful revelation of the love of God that was in operation in the hearts of these saints. I only just managed to sift through the feelings of love to hear the end result. This judgement had come from understanding and the wisdom of God. They were discussing the new arrival's ability to hold the wonders of God and if they were able to cope with the responsibilities that came at each level of the new Kingdom. Many of these new people had little or no knowledge of God on earth and even though these saints wanted them to know the fullness of God here, they were aware that because they had not pursued God on earth, they would not be able to hold the revelation of God that was available at different levels. I remembered those saints that

## A LITTLE PIECE OF HEAVEN

I had met at each level. All of them were content with where they were, even though they were aware that there were other levels. It showed me the tremendous love that these saints had for those that had yet to come to this place and I was overwhelmed with admiration for each of them. I had never seen such concern for an individual's wellbeing.

The lady at my side turned towards me and smiled approvingly, as she could see that I would move on from this door of heaven, with the full knowledge of what it was really about. I was thankful for the opportunity to learn the fullness of what was taking place, rather than leave with a wrong impression.

As I walked away from this door, my guide explained that this was the most important place he could show me before I returned to earth. Many on earth had been confused by the discussions about the book of Revelation which speaks of many rooms in heaven. None of us had any idea what it would mean for those who went to their eternal dwelling place. I now possessed a level of understanding that I could impart to those who thirsted for this knowledge. I knew that I would be on the receiving end of disagreements as I shared my experiences with those on earth. There would be those who would try to prove my revelations wrong, but I was not at all concerned *because there are always people who are not willing to believe.*

# Ministering Spirits, a Golden Door and a Chance Encounter with a Great Man of God

My guide assured me that there were many more doors to pass through and that my journey was far from over.

I walked on and as I walked, I could feel an intensity of the spiritual realm increase. As I looked around I could see wisps of white clouds dancing around me. I continued to walk and I was consumed with an intense peace as ministering spirits surrounded me: spirits who were sent to bless me and fill me with all I needed to continue on to the next door. I remembered many times when I had been on the receiving end of these ministering spirits and loved the feeling of being blessed and encouraged. Most of the time these spirits were sent to me at night and as they ministered I would feel a great sense of peace flood into my body, which would send me into a deep sleep.

My only experience of angels came many years ago. I awoke one morning and even though my eyes were closed, I was aware of something spiritual in front of me. As it got closer, I knew that it was an angel. I did not open my eyes or move a muscle for fear of it going away and I felt such peace as the angel ministered, if only for a matter of moments, before it disappeared.

This time I could see the ministering angels all around me and they were elegant and graceful; I was mesmerised by them. I lost sight of the door I was approaching; all I wanted to do was to sit down and enjoy this experience. My guide had disappeared so I sat down to absorb this angelic sight. I was overwhelmed with feelings of adoration for God as I saw all that He would bring into our lives as we entered this Holy place.

My guide was extremely excited as he ushered me forward to show me the beauty of the next door. He was admiring its appearance more than any other and as I got nearer, I could see why. It was solid gold and encrusted with jewels of every colour. I had never seen anything like it and I wondered why it would be presented in this way. My guide beckoned me to go first and as I passed underneath the frame of the door my whole being was filled with light.

The scene that met me far outweighed the beauty of the door. I could see the saints gathered around, reclining in luxury and enjoying each other's company. I became aware of my physical body being transformed into its perfect state and even though I knew it was temporary I could see that it was better than any earthly body. My skin was the most gorgeous colour and my hair contained many different shades of golden brown and blonde. I felt revitalised and so youthful and as I looked around the room I could see that everyone here had the same renewed body and the same youthfulness. They asked me to sit and join them so that I could share my journey so far.

We discussed the different stages and they were amazed that I was called to return to earth to tell of my time here. They asked me why I thought I was chosen, over so many others. All I could say was that we were living in a new dispensation in which God decided to take many of the saints into the heavenly realms for the purposes of taking back what they had learnt. I told them about the other people I had met and that they were experiencing different aspects of heaven, so that when we returned we could gather together and share all that we had learnt.

As I talked with these saints, I asked them why the door was stunning in comparison to the others I had encountered. They told me that it was the resting place for the saints and it is where most of the ministering angels reside. The treasures of the Kingdom are found here and it is also the place where saints receive their new bodies. Within this place there were many smaller rooms for the saints to visit whenever they wanted to be refreshed with more revelation of the nature of God. It was also a place to share the exploits of the Kingdom and the work that God was doing amongst those He was calling throughout the nations of the world. We could also see the future plans that God revealed to those that would play a specific role in the last days.

As I looked at their faces, I felt that I recognised many that sat in front of me and yet I didn't know why. The more I looked and listened, I realised that these were the saints from the Old and New Testament. I stepped away in shock as I realised I was standing next to Moses. He smiled and reminded me that there was no difference between us. I had so many questions about his life and yet I felt that to sit near him was enough of a privilege. Moses was the humblest man on the face of the earth, (Numbers 12:3). He encouraged me to ask whatever questions I wanted to and so I began;

## A LITTLE PIECE OF HEAVEN

"What stirred your heart after all of those years in Pharaoh's palace to defend your people? After all, you had been amongst the Egyptians since birth."

His reply surprised me.

"Would you ever forget your family and your father's house?"

My next question burst forth.

"How were you so patient when the Israelites were continually sinning and causing all of Israel to remain trapped in the desert for forty years? Why didn't you give up and ask God to release you and your family to another land?"

Moses replied;

"When you are called into your purpose after an encounter with God, you realise that your life is no longer about you. You begin to focus on eternal purposes as you begin to see your life through God's eyes."

I had one last burning question to ask of Moses, and as I breathed a deep breath of courage I asked,

"After forty years of leading the Israelite nation through the desert and then reaching the Promised Land, how did you feel when you were not allowed to enter?"

Moses features remained expressionless; there was no pain and no regret behind his eyes. This great man of God looked like I expected him to look: full of understanding which brought great peace. I believe that this understanding did not only come from his heavenly knowledge of God, but from having walked with God intensely for forty years.

## MINISTERING SPIRITS

And then he spoke:

"I knew you would ask this question, but to understand the answer you have to look deep into your own heart. When God asked me to tap the rock with my stick, He only asked me to do it once. On doing it twice, God saw my heart; I had begun to believe in a power that I possessed, rather than remaining in the place of humility that I had once been: with an acknowledgment that it was all God's power and I had none. God will not share His glory with another and I had come as far as I could with His people, before not only I but they, began to glorify me instead of God. God, in His grace, took me before I entered the Promised Land, in which He knew the people would have tried to raise me up to a place of kingship. A place where pride would have entered my heart, as it had done after hitting the rock more than once. The humility I once had, had left me in that split second and so God in His grace took me before the contamination of sin took hold. I am thankful to God for His mercy and grace upon me and that He took me when He did. I would rather share an eternity of blessings for accomplished works than to remain and fall prey to sin."

As he finished, I could see the overwhelming love that Moses had towards God. I saw that God was more concerned with the state of my heart than anything else. If the humblest man that ever walked the earth could fail in the area of pride, there was no hope for anyone else.

I thanked God for the cross and His Son Jesus Christ. I thanked Moses for his time and his honesty and I continued to walk amongst these amazing people. I met some extraordinary people who had many wonderful stories of their exploits in God, but I decided to keep my questions to a minimum as I would have eternity to ask them.

As I walked through the masses of people that were on this level of heaven, I realised that none of us will ever know what it takes to live a life worthy of being here. Our hearts can deceive us, but they don't deceive God. It is only He that is the judge of all that we have done or will do. *He* is the only One, that weighs our motives and yet we cannot fret over our heart responses in life. We simply must remember that we are on a journey in which our souls are continually being restored and made new in Christ.

I continued to walk through the sea of faces, expectantly waiting to meet more people with amazing stories of faith in God. I was focused on this time in heaven and I wanted it to be all that God intended it to be. I wanted to take back all that I had learnt and pass it on to those that needed to hear. I treasured every conversation and every revelation and I could feel my mind was being transformed with the new things I was learning. Every conversation had changed my mind about aspects of our earthly lives and I could see how limited my thinking had previously been. I had sat under the teaching of great men and women of God and yet I was finding out the limitations of their preaching because of lack of knowledge. It had taken a journey to heaven for me to have a greater understanding of the ways of God.

The frustration that appeared upon the face of my guide spoke louder than any words.

"The treasures of the Kingdom are available to all of those that truly want to find them. Men dig the earth to find diamonds. How much more valuable are the treasures of the Kingdom and yet God's people devote little time to seeking them."

## MINISTERING SPIRITS

I had not sought God enough for these treasures and to be able to stand in this place and have revelations of great truths of God, far exceeded my expectations. As I looked around I could see many of the people getting up and leaving. In fact they were all leaving and they all were going in the same direction. My guide called me to quickly follow, but I didn't want to move on again, as I had become quite comfortable in this place. My natural inclination was to remain in a place of comfort and consequently I became disgruntled when God moved me on, but out of curiosity I followed my guide through the crowds of people to the front of the line.

Suddenly, a cheer erupted from the front and rippled to the back. I couldn't move fast enough, as I wanted to be in full view of this moment and as I was dragged forward by my guide, I could see a lady coming through the gold door that I had come through earlier. The clapping and the shouting that greeted her were deafening and as the crowds surrounded her, a select few slapped her on the back saying, "Well done, well done." She was ushered into the centre of the crowd, onto a regal looking chair.

A chorus of the most beautiful heavenly voices began to sing this lady's favourite song. It was sung by relatives and friends who congratulated her as she was given the crown of life. One of the people in the crowd stepped forward and stood on a podium and unravelled a scroll of gold parchment paper. The saint read this lady's accomplishments and tears of joy ran down her face, as she had forgotten most of the things that were being mentioned. Many of her accomplishments were for obedience shown in what she would have considered small things. You could see the look of disbelief as the works of service were spoken out; she gasped and cried tears of joy with an incredible sense of relief to be in this place. Many of her achievements in Christ were in the area of prayer, most of which took place in her home, behind closed doors. She delighted in her crown of life but the strongest emotion I saw was one of relief and a joy that she would no longer have to carry the burden of prayer. It should have been a light burden, but I could see that like many, she found it difficult to carry her compassion for the lost lightly. *The rewards we receive in heaven are for obedience to the Lord, not for carrying heavy responsibilities that we have accepted from man.*

As I pondered this for my own life, I remembered a number of times when I battled with feelings of not being effective, until God spoke to me on one particular occasion and made it clear that I was to only do what He asked. *We remain more peaceful and consequently more effective when our mind remains uncluttered and more able to hear the voice of the One who leads us.*

This lady was delighted with her rewards and yet she spoke of feelings of inadequacy in her Christian life. She said that being at this place in heaven was a shock. She was surrounded by the saints for many more hours as they made sure they greeted her properly. It was wonderful to see so many genuinely rejoicing over her being here. Her friends and family members would not leave her alone and were at her side for many hours. I could see that just like me, she had many questions and could not stop asking them for a long time. Most of her questions were directed at those she knew, until she started to recognise the saints of Scripture. I saw her go off into the distance with one of the saints of the New Testament, knowing that her her time would be very precious with this special lady.

My guide encouraged me to enjoy the food and

# MINISTERING SPIRITS

fellowship with the saints, as we sat at each other's feet, laughing and chatting. The food was amazing and the fruit and vegetables were unrecognisable with their unique flavours and spices. I thought that fellowship on earth was enjoyable, but it was nothing like what I was experiencing here. People ministered love from one to another with the fruits of the Spirit flowing amongst us. I could actually feel my soul being continually renewed as we talked and laughed.

The more I watched how fellowship should be, the more I became aware of how difficult I was going to find it as I settled back into what I had been used to. How could I go back to enjoying anything after experiencing a much better life here?

My guide suddenly appeared at my side and spoke gently into my ear.

"You have experienced what is possible for the saints in the heavenly realms so that when you return you can teach others how to worship and how to encounter God in many different ways. People are boxed in by religion and those who believe they have great freedom, can still go further than their earthly minds allow. This is the whole purpose of you being here. You will continually be teaching those that you meet a greater truth because of the knowledge you have gained in the heavenly realms."

I felt proud to be used in such a way with the Body of Christ. All I had to do on returning to earth was to listen to God, guiding me in all things and to be careful to seek His wisdom and understanding.

# Angels on Assignment

My guide told me that it was time to leave so that I could continue my journey through heaven. I thanked my friends for a wonderful time of fellowship as I walked back through the gold door, which seemed less impressive after encountering the glory of this room in heaven. As my mind began to spin with all of this knowledge, my guide took me further into the depths of the Kingdom. I wondered how much more I could be shown in this place. My guide assured me that I could not possibly comprehend a fraction of all that was here. I wondered if my fellow travellers would be visiting the places that I had walked past.

I felt drawn to a number of doors and as I stood in front of them, my guide hurried me on. I had learnt so much by going through just one of these doors; I was glad I had an eternity to take in all that was here. Finally, we came to a standstill and stood in front of the plainest looking door of them all; it was one which I would have walked past. My guide smiled as he knew my thoughts; he began to speak about the overwhelming weakness of mankind and their tendency to be drawn by the flesh instead of being led by the Spirit.

As we walked through the door, I became aware of the presence of many angelic beings surrounding us on every side. I had encountered many saints on this level, but this was the first time I had encountered so many angels. They were beautiful and majestic: there was something special about these particular angels, which I had yet to find out. As I walked forward, they ushered me in the direction they wanted me to go. It felt as though they had been waiting for me with a sense of anticipation at what I would see here; nothing was obvious at this stage. God's presence was heavy in this place.

One of the angels took my hand and we pushed ahead into a room which was covered with shelves. As I looked on these shelves I could see vague representations of body parts, which were waiting to be claimed by those who needed them. There was no physical life in these parts but there was spiritual life in them because they were connected in the spirit realm with the people that needed to claim them. I had never seen anything like it, nor did I imagine I ever would. I turned to look for my guide, who had gone, but then appeared out of nowhere. He gently spoke words of peace over me to calm me down as I was overwhelmed by this scene. I had not expected to see a room that contained body parts and I had so many questions.

My guide interrupted my thoughts:

"This is a special place, which is watched over day and night by the same angels. They are angels of creative miracles that God uses to bring the body parts to those in need. These angels are attentive to their task and they continually intercede for faith to increase. Many people's faith cannot comprehend that God would do this for them, so the angels intercede for their faith to grow to the point that they are then able to receive their healing, and the door of doubt is firmly closed.

"Some of the angels are here to deliver the part that is needed and when the healing minister prays, the angel immediately responds by taking the body part to the person, rejoicing as they go for those that receive them. These parts have been waiting here for years. God wants to heal. But faith must be in operation."

I had never seen anything like this. I was overcome with emotion for those that had not received what was already theirs, simply because they did not have the faith to believe that it would happen to them. I looked at the angels; I could see that they were proud of the role they played in this place and were blessed to be a part of the rejoicing as people received what was already theirs. I needed to sit and ponder this wonderful scene so I sat at the feet of the nearest angel, who told me not to be sad, but to rejoice in the knowledge of God's heart towards mankind: knowing that one day all of mankind will have new bodies that will last for eternity.

As the angels moved around the body parts, they prayed for them to be received by those who needed them. It really was a moving scene: I was beginning to see the limitations I had placed on God as far as healing was concerned.

My guide told me to move on to allow the angels to show me another room which was connected to this one but contained a different type of healing. As I moved forward, I could see another door and as it swung open before me, I could see it was a room of healing, but this time it was dedicated to emotional healing. The angels were praying for the saints on earth, to get to a place, where they could receive healing. They also prayed for their Christian foundations to be strong enough to keep it. I understood the need for strong foundations to be in place, after experiencing my own emotional healing as a young Christian. The enemy whispered, "Are you sure it's gone?" And as I crumbled with fear on the inside, the fear came back. It took another three years, before I could claim what was rightfully mine and be strong enough to believe that the enemy had no right in that area of my life.

I could see that the angels were interceding on behalf of those on earth who needed emotional healing. Many had been scarred for a long time and were convinced that the scars were part of their character. I could see their passion for those who were due for a breakthrough and had been seeking God for what they knew they needed. I wondered why it was taking so long before they received their healing.

My guide took me to one side:

"Many who know they need healing are so scarred by their experiences that it takes time to deposit the different aspects of what they need into their life. God cannot work too quickly because they will not be able to cope, so God has to prepare them for the changes. With many of the changes, comes a period of suffering which unearths the part in them that has to go. For every good thing that is waiting to be deposited, there is a stronghold of the enemy that needs to be removed. This process of removal takes time as well as love and understanding.

"Many of God's children do not want to participate in this process of change and this is why you see so many emotional healings waiting to be received. It takes faith for the body parts to be received. But this type of healing takes courage by those that trust God to take them on a journey of change. This change is intense in the early days of their Christianity and many do not want to go through with it.

For those who want to change there are great rewards not only in this life, but in their life to come."

I was glad that my own journey of yielding completely to God started early on in my Christian life. I had already gone through many changes that were necessary for God to use me in the way that He had planned.

I looked at all of the emotional breakthroughs that were yet to be claimed. I could see that many of my brothers and sisters in Christ were trying to live out their Christian lives, without the freedom that was necessary to enable them to be more effective. I thought about many that needed to replace fear with love, which would then enable them to go on to do great works. I could see that without this deliverance from fear, the saints would be unable to move forward in any area of their life. *If we could only see what we could achieve in Christ by yielding our lives more fully to God! This would create growth and maturity, rather than comfort and security.*

As I passed through this room, I was shown the emotions yet to be received, with forgiveness taking prime position on every shelf. I could not believe that this gift had not been claimed by so many. I had received this gift into my heart many times as I made a choice to forgive and to bless. The gift I received was the Fathers forgiveness.

"For if you forgive men when they sin against you, your heavenly Father will also forgive you. But if you do not forgive men their sins, your Father will not forgive your sins."

Matthew 6:14-15

*To forgive is difficult for many people – especially those*

## A LITTLE PIECE OF HEAVEN

*that have been on the receiving end of abuse and all sorts of other awful acts brought about by mankind. God cannot fill us with His love if there is anger, bitterness or simply unforgiveness in its place. It is similar to a glass being full of milk and someone is waiting to fill it with water. Until we pour one substance away (and forgive) God cannot fill us with His love. We are either left with one or the other. There is a period of time that we are under God's grace when these awful things happen to us, but there comes a time when it is time to forgive. When we refuse to forgive we can suffer from a number of effects, one of which is depression. God is waiting to bring His fullness into the lives of His children. He is a God who wants to deposit the good and perfect gifts of His Kingdom in all of those that are ready to receive His love. But unforgiveness cannot reside with His love; the two simply will not cohabit.*

The angels retreated from me until one of them, took hold of my hand and guided me to a table where an emotional healing was waiting to be received by a person on earth. The angel asked if I would like to go and watch as this emotion was deposited. I willingly accepted this invite and was immediately whisked away in the Spirit through the heavens, to a church meeting that was taking place on the earth.

This meeting was attended by masses of people and as I entered into the spiritual atmosphere, I could see that God was here in a way I had not previously encountered on earth. The God of compassion and healing was in our midst and He was giving the souls of His people much needed restoration. The angel told me to stand next to a lady who had wanted to be healed of depression for many years. Her heart had been broken when her youngest child had been abducted and abused and she had never been able to forgive those that had committed this awful crime. At the moment we arrived, the anointed speaker was sharing her own loss and a similar story of losing a child through abduction and death. The power of her testimony was that she was able to forgive, which resulted in an instantaneous healing of her broken heart. The healing in turn led to the restoration of her marriage and the healing of physical problems. As she shared the story, the Spirit of God moved upon this lady's heart and she broke down.

We arrived at the moment of decision. The lady fell to her knees and I heard her cry "I forgive". As the tears streamed down her face, the angel took me to her side and asked me to place my hand upon her heart, assuring me that the lady could not see me. I reached forward and the angel told me to deposit the gift of forgiveness into her heart. As I did this, I could feel the presence of God deposit the gift that was hers. She fell down and collapsed in a heap of tears and as she did this, I could see her face change. It was no longer distorted with pain; the ageing process that had taken its toll appeared to reverse and a youthful glow took its place.

We stayed for a while longer. I simply watched visible changes take place as many gathered around her to continue praying. Arms surrounded her, but they were not the arms of people: they were the arms of the One that had waited so long to give her the gift that was hers and to set her on a journey of change. God was going to use this lady in healing many that had been through similar suffering. The angel motioned that it was time to leave and before I could think anything else, I found myself back in the heavenly realms in awe at what had just happened.

My guide was waiting for me:

"So you see: God is always waiting to give good gifts to

His children. He doesn't withhold, unless He has good reason."

*I had more of an understanding of why we were taught to praise God in all circumstances. By doing this we are proclaiming in faith that we utterly believe that God's love for us will bring victory through His goodness that is always at work. We must not assume what He will do, or when or how He will do it: we simply must believe that the outcome of our lives will be all that God wants it to be. Our understanding is the only thing that gets in the way. We must lay down our lack of understanding and replace it with faith in the One that will always work on our behalf to achieve His purposes, in and through our lives.*

As I rejoined the angels, they began to sing praises to God for the lady that had just received forgiveness and emotional healing; she had been released from ten years of pain.

Someone was in our midst that I recognised. It was Jesus! He danced wildly and weaved His way through the angels of creative miracles. These were the ones who had worked with Jesus since the beginning of the world and the bond between them was great. He danced and danced with such great excitement and I started to dance with Him. Jesus took my hand and He gently guided me to another realm of heaven. As He did this, I was taken up to a higher place where the angels sang the loveliest of songs; they began to worship in a way that I had not heard before. Each sang a new song which harmonised beautifully, causing us to dance and express our love towards the God of the ages. These songs unearthed an inspiration to dance in new and creative ways. I found myself being able to naturally express my worship with each move being unique.

I did not realise that these new moves of dance were not only a visual display of worship alone. With each move came power to release those in bondage. As I moved, it felt like electricity was passing through my body and leaving me as the move was complete. God showed me that this type of dancing was going to be expressed in the last days for those that needed healing. I could see that creative gifts were going to become powerful conduits of healing.

As I danced, I was given the ability to see the type of healing that would manifest. I could see that, in the last days, ministries would be released upon the earth in ways previously unseen. It would require a people that were completely sold out to the purposes of God and only those without inhibitions, who had been completely set free from the fear of man. As I danced, those that joined me displayed incredible power, which emanated from their bodies. I had to stop and observe all that was taking place. I was beginning to see the reality of the Scripture that tells us that we will do greater works than Jesus. Although there was a long way to go before Christians would bring the full expression of God upon the earth.

"I tell you the truth, anyone who has faith in me will do what I have been doing. He will do even greater things than these, because I am going to the Father."

### John 14:12

The Lord appeared in front of me and spoke of the last days of the glory that would be poured into the lives of those who had yielded to His purposes. He spoke of the ministries that would be released: no longer would churches suppress those with a particular gift for fear of offence or looking foolish. Those that suppressed the servant of Christ in the last days would be removed from their position and only those that would allow God's ministers to operate freely would be allowed to stand in the last days. The Lord spoke of the judgements for those that suppress the gifts and how He had longed for those He had called to be recognised in the Body of Christ. The Lord spoke His heart clearly;

"Until My church recognises the people that I have sent with particular gifts that will bless, build up and encourage the body; My people cannot properly be joined together with powerful ministries in the last days. The more the churches resist those that seem different or threatening, the less I can achieve in their midst. To resist those I send is to resist Me."

The Lord only spoke to me when He was particularly passionate about seeing His heart for people released on the earth. So I vowed that I would do my best to remember all of these moments in particular and pray that they would be worked out in my life and the life of the church.

He turned and walked away and I could see that He had expressed a very short but powerful declaration about His desire in the last days for those He would send to the nations. It was the same passion that Jesus had displayed to His disciples who were all sent with a task to preach the Gospel message and to achieve His purpose.

I felt that I had seen all that I was meant to see in this place in heaven, even though I could have seen so much more. My guide led me away from this scene towards a new dimension of heaven.

# The Garden of Remembrance

As I was led away, my guide bowed to acknowledge and honour my place in God because I had been taken to an area in heaven rarely shown to anyone. I felt such honour at being allowed to see all that I had and I wondered what I had done to be so privileged to enter this place. I quickly remembered what I had been told earlier by God, that it was not about recognition; I was simply chosen. Even so, I could not help but feel honoured to be chosen and I could see that my guide felt privileged to be chosen to bring me here. We walked away and as we walked, I could see those that had previously entered the heavenly realms. It was as if paintings of them were all around me as I saw them in the Spirit; I was then told that I would be added to the collection upon leaving here.

I walked for a long time with my guide and he showed me a place to sit and rest to ponder the day's events. I recognised this place and yet I didn't know why. It was a garden and it was beautiful with every leaf coloured with the most exquisite shades of green. When I saw something of beauty, I had a tendency to stare, sometimes with my jaw slightly agape, especially if I was in awe of the scene. I found it difficult to believe that I would take this stance over a colour of a leaf; yet

## A LITTLE PIECE OF HEAVEN

here I was staring at it.

As I looked around this lovely garden, I realised that it was not just any garden; this was the Garden of Eden. But how could I be in a garden that existed over two thousand years ago? I was overwhelmed with a desire to visit the tree of the knowledge of good and evil. I looked around the garden and as the streams wound their way around the flower beds, the sunshine bounced off the leaves that had recently been sprayed with morning dew. The reflection of the trees in the water mirrored the beauty of this place and as I walked the birdsong enhanced all that was here.

I then realised that I wouldn't recognise the tree - even if I walked into it. Or would I? I wanted to enjoy all that was before me and so I sat down to absorb the beauty of the garden and wondered why Adam and Eve would have wanted more than what they had here. I thought about my own life and the times I had become dissatisfied, which led me to thoughts that took me away from God and His wonderful presence. *When we believe the lie that God alone is not enough, we fall from grace. It is sad that as human beings we continually fall for this lie. We chase rainbows hoping to find our pot of gold only to find we end up chasing yet another one. We are never satisfied and are always left hungry for more.* This place had everything you could ever want. The supply of food was varied and never-ending with fruit hanging off every tree and bush. Everywhere I looked there were trees and bushes that supplied a wide variety of every food type. I looked up to see a willow tree unusually bearing fruit and as I reached out to taste its fruit, I bit into its yellow and pink flesh. My tongue came alive with a variety of flavours; all of them sweet. The juices ran down my chin and onto my clothes; I could not stop devouring this delicious fruit.

## THE GARDEN OF REMEMBRANCE

I bent down and grabbed the fruit of a bush in front of me and I was pleasantly surprised to find that this fruit had a savoury taste to it. I was not expecting this from fruit! Every fruit or vegetable I picked contained flavours I had not tasted before and was far better than any on earth. After having my fill, I quickly forgot that I had been seeking the tree of knowledge and I fell into a deep sleep beneath a quaint looking cherry tree.

My sleep developed into a dream in which I was taken out of my body and in front of the tree of knowledge. All I could see was a fine mist surrounding a tree that stood alone; outstanding in its beauty. Its branches looked ominous and frightening and I could not see the same beauty that was evident in the trees of the Garden of Eden. It had a kingly beauty, which towered over me threateningly. There were no leaves; the bark was dark and bleak with a beauty that came from within. This beauty had the power to heal the nations.

I was afraid and I wondered if this really was the tree of the knowledge of good and evil because I could feel nothing but darkness. It felt as though the power within the tree was getting into my soul. I stepped back and cried out to God for His protection and as I did this, angelic beings came out of nowhere. They flew in front of the tree from left to right, with their swords thrashing and cutting at an invisible force that came from the heart of the tree. As they did this, light forced its way from the back of the tree. This light was a separate entity from the tree itself and was forcing the tree to submit to the goodness wrapped up within.

A battle ensued and the forces of good and evil raged within the core of the tree. The tree shook with the power at work within: its roots creaked and moved up and out of the ground, revealing a fresh layer of root on the surface. It seemed as though the tree could not stand much more of the pressures within and I wondered how much of this pressure it had withstood up to this point. As I looked closer at the trunk of the tree, I could see that it had aged in the time I had stood there; this tree was as old as time itself and for it to have lasted until now was incredible.

But this was no ordinary tree: it signified the downfall of mankind. Within its bark were the secrets of the last days of the Kingdom of light and upon its surface the pain of its fall into darkness. I stood in front of the most infamous landmark in all mankind, one which would forever remind us of the fall of man. I stood back to see the tree being consumed by light; it shone so brightly, that I could no longer look at it.

My spirit returned to my body and I was asleep under the cherry tree.

I awoke to the shrill sound of the blackbird above me; it was time to welcome the new day and all that it had in store. The cherry blossom looked magnificent and to be able to lie underneath it in the most temperate of climates; whilst being surrounded by food that satisfied every taste, made me not want to move. The most wonderful sense of satisfaction entered my soul as the blossom fell and a gentle breeze blew across my face. I thought about the day that Adam and Eve looked for the tree of knowledge. Had they become dissatisfied with all that they had been given *before* they reached this tree? Or was it simply that sin entered their heart when the enemy tempted them with thoughts of having something more than what God had already given them? I remembered my dream the night before and as I went over the different events, I could see that the tree was shaken to the core at certain times of the day, when evil raged within. For the remainder of the day the tree remained at peace as goodness took its place. It was only when the angelic beings battled, to prevent evil leaving the tree, that the tree was aware that its days were numbered and that good would eventually prevail.

I remembered how old the bark of the tree looked and the darkness that was wrapped up inside of it. I could tell that the battles that were continually taking place on the earth, resulted in a continual shaking in this heavenly tree of knowledge. I understood why I could only see the darkness of this tree instead of its light. With the fall of man the knowledge of good had been swallowed up by the knowledge of evil. This was an exact representation of the world we lived in. The only thing that stopped the tree being swallowed up completely by evil was the warring angels sent periodically by God to keep evil at bay. The angels will wage this war until the final trumpet sounds the victory of good over evil. *This victory has already been won through the death of Jesus, but it has yet to come into fullness in the lives of those He came to save. Until it does the battle will continue.*

I could see why I had been shown this in a dream: God wanted to show me how Adam and Eve had fallen from being perfect human beings into sinful ones; when enticed by Satan himself. I had been shown the tremendous pull of evil that was contained in the tree and I saw why God specifically asked Adam and Eve, not to taste its fruit. The fruit of this tree was knowledge and this knowledge had the power to destroy all of those that encountered it. Thankfully, the angelic hosts were sent to rescue me; without their intervention I would have been enticed just as Adam and Eve were. I thought about this moment in the lives of Adam and Eve and wondered if they also had encountered the angelic host who warred for their souls. The difference was that they were without sin and so should not have encountered the same intense battle.

Wisdom spoke within me and showed me that *for man to truly be complete, the decision not to sin must be purely their own. Until man understands God's complete love for them, they will always be fighting in this area of doubt.* As wisdom spoke this to me, I understood God's unfailing love for His people. I could see that people would only follow God wholeheartedly when they were convinced that there was no better way.

I rose to my feet and walked around the garden to explore all that should have been ours. I could see that many of God's people would have spent a lot of time enjoying creation, tending the flowers and looking after the fruit and vegetables. There would have been little competition in this place and little or no time for thinking only of oneself, as it was a place of generosity.

It was a place in which the people would have no desire to improve their standard of living because everything they needed was here. A lot of time would have been spent in fellowship, one with another, with thoughts to bless others, rather than look to our own needs. I tried adjusting to thoughts of a new lifestyle as I wandered around this perfect place in heaven; I struggled with thoughts of empty days. I had no idea of the plans of God in this place and after a life of many battles, the pressures of life and bringing up children. I was left wondering how I would fill my days in this place of perfection.

My guide appeared at my side as he perceived my thoughts:

"After one day of seeing all that there is to see in this

# THE GARDEN OF REMEMBRANCE

place, everyone asks the same question. Those who have spent their time on earth going from one drama of life to the next, or those who have been busy with work commitments and bringing up children, can feel that their lives here would be empty. People thrive on being busy with their lives; it results in a feeling of self-worth. God's people should learn to remain in a place of being satisfied with His presence. This is one of the most difficult lessons for all of God's people and many have not learnt to do this. Once this has been achieved, His people are much more effective for the Kingdom, because they are operating out of His presence and peace to do the things that He requires.

"Competition will go; selfish ambition will go; boredom will go, as will the continuous struggle to find activities that bring you a sense of wellbeing. Many of God's people do not realise that those things done for the wrong reasons will be burnt up on entering heaven. Only those things that have been done because of the will of the Father will remain. Many of God's people forfeit what could be theirs for fear of losing their worldly life and fleshly ambition. But when they let go of their desires, they will find that they are given so much more in this life and the next.

> "For whoever wants to save his life will lose it, but whoever loses his life for me will find it."
>
> Matthew 16:25

"Those that truly follow Jesus will find that their whole life will be called into question and the only work that remains will be that which bears fruit. When His children understand that God is their portion and that only He

# A LITTLE PIECE OF HEAVEN

can fill their lives with satisfaction, they will then receive all that is theirs in Jesus Christ. They will move into areas of gifting, that they never thought possible. Many of God's children will be moved into supernatural gifting. These areas of gifting will bring great fruit and they will be amazed at His work in their lives. Saying this, there are few that take this path; it is a lonely one. It is a path in which God turns everything you have known upside down so that you feel that you are on the wrong side of the fence. But it's worth it!"

I could see that the years I had spent learning to rely on God to meet all of my needs, whether spiritually or emotionally, had reaped their rewards and as I entered heaven my attitude would be one of resting in His presence. I was developing a deep desire for entering the rest of God and as I took one more look at paradise; my guide encouraged me to walk on. I could see that we would all love this place of provision and we would easily adjust to the peace and provision that God had intended for all of His children. Clouds gathered around us which made my last views of the garden fade abruptly. I was not sure where my guide was going to take me next and my mind was so full of the Garden of Eden that I did not want to think of anything else.

# A Place of Regret and Triumph!

I had been taken to the highest place in heaven and shown more than I had ever dreamt possible. The Garden of Eden was in the highest place in heaven because it was a place of perfect provision for God's children. The second and third places of heaven were created because of sin and they were only created for those who could not hold the fullness of His glory on entering heaven. My thought life was being renewed and as each new revelation of heaven was revealed; my outlook on life was changing. I wanted God to use me to bring people into a greater understanding of God and His ways; so I was glad for these profound changes.

As I walked through the clouds, I felt as though I was being lifted higher: a floating sensation took over. I floated above the garden and above all that I had previously been shown in the higher realms of heaven. Even though I was in the Spirit, it was a surreal experience because I was taken through heaven in such a short time. I then found myself quickly descending and going deeper and deeper into the depths of the earth. Fear gripped me as I descended to a place that I was not ready to see. I shouted to my guide to stop and I wanted to either return to earth or to revisit heaven.

My guide looked at me and shouted;

## A LITTLE PIECE OF HEAVEN

"I thought you wanted to go into all of the heavenly realms. This might not be heaven in the sense of angels and God but all of heaven, earth and hell belongs to God. To get a full revelation and understanding of all of who God is, you must visit hell, if only for a moment. Even Jesus, passed through this place."

I was not happy and I started to fret and panic until my guide grabbed hold of my hand and I could feel the strength and peace of God pour into my soul. Thankfully, these feelings were so overwhelming that I was able to submit to the purpose for which God had called me. I went into the darkest recesses of the earth. Blackness surrounded us and I could not see a thing; fear did not seem to enter my heart, but only because the Lord was protecting me. I walked forward with my guide, who assured me that nothing bad was going to happen and that I was only here to observe. I entered a room which I could see was a waiting room for those that had just died. I saw many that were seated in this place and were in complete silence and utter shock at being here. What saddened my heart was that there were many here that refused to believe in either heaven or hell and as they were given the choice to believe (while they were dying) they still managed to resist God. They refused because of pride; they could not accept they had gone throughout their lives without the knowledge of God. The reasons for them doing this were varied, for some it was pride and for others it was that they could not face the fact that their relatives and friends might not be in heaven with them.

What I was seeing should have caused me to crumble and the pain I would normally have felt would have been unbearable, but I was being protected from this. As these people sat in the waiting room, they were called

# A PLACE OF REGRET AND TRIUMPH!

one by one to face their life and to face the God they should have served. Each one had the opportunity to receive forgiveness and salvation and yet for reasons beyond my understanding, there were many whose hearts would not yield. I could only guess that their hearts were so embroiled with sin, that they could not even hear the voice of Grace as their embittered souls refused forgiveness. I was not sure why I was here and I couldn't wait to leave. With nowhere to run, I was forced into viewing this awful scene.

Even in this place God existed, with judgement and grace for all who submitted to Him. I thought of those I had lost and who had not become Christians before they died and I wondered what had become of them as they entered this place. Surely, their hearts were not so calloused that they would not have received the grace that was theirs. My guide turned to me and reminded me that only God knows what is hidden in the hearts of man.

All of a sudden, light broke through the darkness into the room and a shaft of light was shed upon one of those waiting. The light of God was so bright upon them that I could not understand how anyone could fail to respond to it and welcome God with open arms. This light could not penetrate the heart of the person unless the person yielded to the light. The heart of the person in front of me must have been like the blackest coal and the hardest iron and I found it difficult to believe that they would ever make a decision to allow the light of God in. However I could see softness begin to appear in their face as the light of God broke into their soul. They were whisked away into the heavenly realms. No words were spoken as the person received the forgiveness that was theirs; all they had to do was acknowledge in their heart that the Son of God was their Saviour and they were transported into the kingdom of light. Hell split apart as it released them from its evil grasp and then returned to its blackened state. I could see from this that the heart of God would never give up calling those that were His, right until their last breath and beyond the grave. God does everything in His power, to bring His children home and I wondered why so many resisted His love, even when faced with the vilest of punishments.

As I looked up, I could see the cross of Christ, in a vision hovering above this scene. My heart grew sad, as I saw the love of God bursting through this awful place. Wherever I had been on my journey in heaven, God's love was at the forefront and there was nowhere that His love couldn't reach. I was so moved at this scene, that just for a moment, even though in hell, all I could see was the love of God displayed through Calvary, when the ultimate price was paid for mankind.

My guide turned to me and beckoned me forward to take a look at another side of hell. As I walked forward, I suddenly became aware that I was just about to step off a cliff into hell's throat. I teetered on the edge, trying to gain my balance; wanting to get away from this place as quickly as possible. The edge of the cliff crumbled and as I scrambled to gain my balance, I had just enough time to peer into hell and the place of passing through. I had the feeling that even at this point, as hell loomed, many were saved and whisked into the heavenly realms as the grace of God hung on until the last moment. God waited for His children to acknowledge, His Son, Jesus and the power of His blood to bring salvation to their souls.

As the flames licked the base of my feet, I could not help but scream out to my guide, who quickly came to my aid. As I fell back, God showed me many that had teetered on the edge of His kingdom of light and the

## A PLACE OF REGRET AND TRIUMPH!

kingdom of darkness all of their lives. He showed me how He had sent His children to rescue them. Many had received Jesus into their heart and then after a season, they allowed the pleasures of the world to entice them away from God. *The biggest deception the enemy uses is to make unbelievers think that the world has more to offer. Life can only be experienced in all its fullness when the life of God is within us, through the workings of His Holy Spirit. What many don't realise is that they are dead in their sin and they cannot truly start to live a life of joy and peace until they submit to God.*

The pit that I was now seeing caused me to shudder with fear and just for a moment, God allowed me to see all that I had been saved from. I fell to my knees in the middle of hell to worship the One who saves. As I fell, my life flashed before my eyes and the many things I had done, my un-repented sin, stared me in the face. It was only when deep repentance took hold of my heart that I asked for forgiveness. Some of these things were small in my eyes and yet they had a tremendous effect on the lives of those around.

Remorse and regret took root in my heart and the tears gave way to uncontrollable sobbing. My guide took me gently by the hand and told me that I didn't have to go through any more than this and that I had been forgiven already. He showed me that God's purposes for me, meant that I had to see this place to enable me to take it back and share with those God brought along my path. For a moment I was lost in my regret, until I realised that I did not have to go through these emotions because of the blood of Christ that was shed to cleanse me from my sins. My guide reminded me that *we must all eventually go before the judgement seat of Christ but that it was nothing to fear*. I was relieved (to say the least) and I quickly rose to my feet to receive the cleansing from these awful dark emotions.

As my guide rushed me away from this place, he told me that he could not warn me of this impending trauma because it would have made it much worse, but he was sorry to have had to be the one to take me through it. His arm surrounded me and he kissed me on the top of my head, as if he was saying, "If I could, I would have saved you from seeing this place". *And I believe that this is what God would say to all of mankind.*

The awful feelings were replaced with the lightness of the presence of God, as the glory of His salvation burned brightly in my heart. I was glad that I had been through many places in heaven but to truly understand it, I had to experience hell.

I yearned for my home on earth, even though I knew that one day heaven would be my home. But for now I could not settle here, as my purpose on earth was not complete. An incredible hunger for the purposes of God had been birthed in my heart and soul, not only for me, but for those Jesus came to save and to align with His eternal purpose. My guide took me to rest from the day's events and I was again surrounded by many who had been experiencing heaven as I had. It was good to see them and know that we had been taken through similar places in heaven. It was just what I needed to take my mind off the day's events. Not one of us mentioned our time in hell as we knew we would relive it if we did.

A feast had been prepared for all of us and we were told that it was going to be a time of great celebration in heaven as we had each completed our time here. None of us had any idea that our time for leaving had arrived and yet we each discussed feeling extreme longings to be reunited with loved ones on the earth. We could see that

## A PLACE OF REGRET AND TRIUMPH!

God had saved our journey to hell until the end in order to produce the necessary longing to return to earth. God wanted us to hunger for His purposes above all else and this was the signal for our return.

We looked around and saw that for this occasion, all the saints of heaven had gathered to celebrate our being here and for our fruitfulness as we returned to earth. The dancing and the celebrations went on for many hours: for many of us this would be our last memory as we left for home. The food that had been prepared was outstanding in its preparation and appearance; it really was fit for a King. Suddenly there was a sounding of trumpets and a clash of drums. A drum roll signalled the entrance of the King and the angelic hosts prepared the way with rose petals strewn at His feet. The smell was idyllic and the fragrance caused us all to be silent as we awaited His entrance to the celebrations.

I imagined Jesus appearing in royal robes, but I was surprised when His attire was no different to the last time I saw Him. A simple white robe, with a gold rope tied around His waist. I saw a crown of thorns upon His head, but this time it was gold with beads of solid gold dropping down and lightly touching His forehead. Each bead symbolised the pain that turned to gold for those He came to save. Barefooted, this almighty King walked into the celebrations and I wept tears of joy as I was given a glimpse of the celebrations that would be held on the final day. In fact, we all wept with joy as we were overwhelmed by this wonderful scene.

Jesus walked towards us and we all sat in awe of the One who came to earth, the One who heals all of our diseases and brings salvation. I sat down and heard a rush of feet surround the King. An array of dancers dressed in purple began to dance and worship Him and as they weaved their way to the front they threw rose petals at His feet.

As Jesus approached we were consumed with feelings of majesty before our King, causing us to fall down and worship Him.

He then sat with us and asked us to share our stories of heaven; particularly the moments we would treasure the most and what we had learnt that would make a difference to our lives on earth. As you can imagine, this conversation went on for hours as we expressed our delight and our sadness over some of the things we had seen. There was complete silence as we each listened to one another's stories of heaven. Jesus listened intently with such interest and delight as he heard our different reactions to our journey.

We were then asked what impacted us the most and how we would share it with loved ones and those we would meet in the future. We all agreed that we were deeply moved by the fact that wherever we went, Jesus came with us; even into the depths of hell. We all had been instilled with a deep confidence and security that no matter how low a person goes and how far they fall, that there is always a way back, even until the very end.

We all embraced the One who loved us more than we would ever know. The love of Christ became embedded into the depths of our being and we each found ourselves back in the heart of our family on earth. We had a burden to share our story of heaven and hoped that we would meet one another again, to celebrate and share our experiences with those who wanted to listen.

## A PLACE OF REGRET AND TRIUMPH!

"...'Come, I will show you the bride, the wife of the Lamb.' And he carried me away in the Spirit to a mountain great and high, and he showed me the Holy City, Jerusalem, coming down out of heaven from God. It shone with the glory of God, and its brilliance was like that of a very precious jewel, like a jasper, clear as crystal.'"

Revelation 21:9-11

www.ingramcontent.com/pod-product-compliance
Lightning Source LLC
Chambersburg PA
CBHW061646040426
42446CB00010B/1614